Here's what our readers are saying...

The finest, most organized guide I've ever seen! Greatly needed by people seeking job opportunities. The handiness of the book is incredible. It's practical. It's complete. It's as well organized as any I've read.

> Frederick W. Bennetts
> Director of Public Relations (retired)
> Oldsmobile Division
> General Motors Corporation

Mid-Career Changes: Strategies for Success *is a provocative and helpful book, packed with sound advice on how to manage our careers in a world in which the old approaches do not seem to work.*

> John J. Mozeliak
> Director, TeamFocus Centers
> Tascor/IBM Corporation

Mid-Career Changes: Strategies for Success *provides a clear, concise outline for developing a career strategy. It is especially appropriate for individuals trying to deal with unplanned mid-career changes as the result of corporate downsizing. I have already loaned my copy to a close friend who finds himself in such a situation.*

> Theodore K. Barnhart
> Manager, Organization and
> Management Compensation
> Planning,
> Chrysler Corporation

Mid-Career Changes:
Strategies for Success

by
**John D. Shingleton
and James Anderson**

Career Publishing Inc.
Orange, CA

Book & Cover Design: Harris Graphics
Editor/Project Coordinator: Valerie L. Harris
Assistant Editor: Joani C. Saari
Production: Valerie L. Harris, Joani C. Saari

This book was produced by Desktop Publishing techniques
using Microsoft Word, and Aldus PageMaker on
Macintosh computers and output to a LaserMaster 1200.

This publication is designed to provide accurate and authoritative information in regard to the subject matter covered. It is sold with the understanding that the publisher is not engaged in rendering legal, accounting or other professional service. If legal advice or other expert assistance is required, the service of a competent professional person should be sought.

Disclaimer: Information has been obtained by Career Publishing, Inc., from sources believed to be reliable. However, because of the possibility of human or mechanical error by our sources, Career Publishing, Inc., or others, Career Publishing, Inc., does not guarantee the accuracy, adequacy, or completeness of any information and is not responsible for any errors or omissions or the results obtained from the use of such information. The publisher and editors shall not be held liable in any degree for any loss or injury by any such omission, error, misprinting or ambiguity. If you have questions regarding the content of this publication, the editorial staff is available to provide information and assistance.

First Edition 1993
ISBN 0-89262-407-8
Library of Congress Catalog Card Number 93-71651

Published by

Career
PUBLISHING INCORPORATED
VOCATIONAL & APPLIED TECHNOLOGY

910 N. MAIN STREET
ORANGE, CA 92667

PRINTED AND BOUND IN THE UNITED STATES OF AMERICA

National/Canada
1 (800) 854-4014
Includes Alaska, Hawaii
and Puerto Rico

10 9 8 7 6 5 4 3 2 1

Contents

Prologue

Employment trends are changing rapidly. Mergers, corporate downsizing, lay-offs, technology, global competition, early retirement, increased longevity, and the quest for a better life are just a few of the variables affecting today's workers. For these reasons and many others, more people are reevaluating their employment status and looking around to see what else may be available for them.

There is no question that the number of people seeking a mid-career change is increasing. However, the process can be agonizing if you do not approach it properly. Many people rush through the process in an effort to end the transition as quickly as possible, making poor decisions along the way. They don't know how to make the change a positive one. The important thing to remember is that career changes can bring you opportunity or despair. The outcome is all up to you.

If you are like most people, your work is a big part of your life; and when it fails to satisfy your needs, you want to correct the problem—fast! What you need is a plan. A career plan tells you where you are going and how to get there. Then, in order to put your plan into action, you must believe in yourself. The secret is to capitalize on your strengths.

We've found that many people faced with a career change need help. Coping with change is not easy; in fact, many do not know where to start. Whether you are an executive looking for a new career, a retired military officer, a home-maker seeking to enter the job market, someone who is being forced into a career change, or simply a person who is dissatisfied with your current work, this book is designed to give you the direction and strategy you need to reach your goals.

About the Authors

As Director of Placement at Michigan State University for over 25 years, John (Jack) D. Shingleton has advised thousands of students and alumni in planning their careers and placement in the fields of business, industry, government, and education. As founder of *Recruiting Trends*, he has co-authored the publication for 17 years. He also founded the Collegiate Employment Institute.

The author of several career books, Mr. Shingleton served as a weekly career columnist for the *Detroit Free Press* from 1984-1988. He has also participated in the creation of several television documentaries and has appeared on the NBC *Today Show* and the CBS *Morning News* to share his expertise in human resources.

Mr. Shingleton continues to serve as a consultant to various employers in business, industry and education, and is Vice Chairman on the Board of Trustees at Michigan State University. In recognition for his professional contributions, the Midwest College Placement Association recently named its annual outstanding research award after Mr. Shingleton.

James Anderson, President of Anderson & Company, a management consulting firm based in Englewood, Colorado, has over 20 years' experience in human resources. His expertise includes leadership development, executive and managerial recruitment and selection, testing and professional skills assessment, outplacement, development of performance appraisal systems, and organizational development. He has provided consulting services for numerous Fortune 100 clients in the automotive and manufacturing industries and financial institutions, as well as for state agencies, higher education, small and medium-sized service industry firms, and health care providers.

Mr. Anderson has delivered seminars and addresses to executive groups, professional associations, and client groups on leadership, recruitment, and various career and professional development topics. He has also published a number of articles in professional and trade journals on these same subjects. Local and national affiliates of NBC and CBS, as well as radio and newspapers, have interviewed him on several occasions for his opinions on human resource issues.

Acknowledgments

Many hours of hard work and sacrifice have gone into this book in the belief that there are many who, for various reasons, want to make a change in their careers. The information it holds is based on our own experience, and the experiences of countless others who helped sharpen the cutting edge of our message.

To Dr. Patrick Scheetz, Director of the Collegiate Employment Institute at Michigan State University, Dr. William Sederberg, Vice President of Public Sector Consultants, Inc., and Dr. Chester Francke, former Human Resources Executive for General Motors Corporation, we express our sincere appreciation for their suggestions and critique of the manuscript.

To Joanne Lewis for her great help in typing the original manuscript, we offer a special word of thanks.

To Valerie Harris and Joani Saari who edited and produced the book, we are most grateful.

We hope this book will be of benefit to all those seeking their niche in the world of work.

Introduction

There are many methods to making a mid-career change. We all have different needs, different goals, and different measuring sticks of success. There are some common denominators, however, and we can learn from other's experiences, remote as those experiences may be from our own. Here is an example of one man's successful career change.

Richard Evanson owns an island in the South Pacific. As a young boy, he developed a love of nature and the outdoors. Helping his parents in their gardening and spending his summers on his uncle's farm in Oregon, he grew to appreciate working outside and feeling close to nature. Though he was always aware of this interest, the practical requirements of earning money for college, attending college, and the pursuit of business success after graduation led him far from working close to nature.

Richard developed a strong work ethic at an early age. Influenced by industrious parents, he began selling newspapers on the street at the age of eight and progressed to a paper route soon after that. By the time he was in high school, Richard had a regular job as a shoe salesman in a local retail outlet. He worked his way through college as a factory worker. Thus, Richard developed a strong orientation for self-reliance and autonomy.

After earning a bachelor's degree in engineering, Richard applied to the Harvard MBA program. While he maintains the program was difficult for him, he graduated in the top one-third of his class.

Upon graduation from Harvard, Richard could have gone to work for his father-in-law, a CEO of a major corporation. Most of his classmates were applying for positions in corporate settings in order to gain business experience. However, Richard made a bold move. He started his own business with a loan from a major bank.

Defending his decision, Richard says his strong need for self-reliance and autonomy simply would not allow him to take directions from others. Richard had never handled submitting to authority very well. He had always wanted to make it on his own and be his own boss.

Richard's main objective at that time was to make money. Money, he thought, was the only way to get what he wanted in life.

His first attempt at business (a cable television station) was a success. By the age of 30 he was financially independent. However, he adds that he did not really feel fulfilled at this time. He was facing a divorce, drinking heavily, and in some-what of a dilemma over his career. He realized that if he stayed with the cable business, he could increase his already significant net worth many times over. However, like many who consider career change, he simply was not happy with what he was doing and felt a need to leave. That decision would not lead him on an easy path.

At the age of 33, Richard was divorced, drinking heavily, living in an apartment in San Francisco, and losing a lot of money in the stock market. Money continued to be his primary focus. To him, money meant independence and freedom from having to serve or please others. He continued to believe that only money would afford him such security and independence, although his experience with the cable station had already shown him that money, alone, is not enough.

After several bad investments in the stock market, Richard was able to turn the tables. He shifted his investments into real estate, and made (almost by accident) what he considers one of the best decisions of his life. He left the United States and travelled the South Pacific, planning to eventually move to Australia to examine real estate investment opportunities. On his way, he stopped in the Fiji Islands. A real estate broker there was able to interest Richard in a piece of property known as Turtle Island. The broker and Richard flew over the island and without setting foot on the property, Richard purchased it.

Feeling misdirected and insecure about interaction with others, Richard saw the island as a refuge and escape. He hoped the island would provide him with some fun until he sold it for profit. However, on the island Richard learned one of the most important lessons a person involved in a mid-career change may learn.

Richard began to realize how important his love for the outdoors was to him. He decided to make some improvements to the island and build a small resort. As Richard became involved with the resort project, he found that it was far more important to him to preserve the natural beauty of the island than to maximize the income potential of the resort. His improvements focused on protecting the natural setting of the island so that guests could enjoy a true natural paradise.

Richard grew to love the island and sought to provide a unique vacation resort for guests. Working outdoors allowed him to be close to nature—a setting with which he was comfortable. Furthermore, the project also allowed him to retain his independence.

The island is not an obsession; but, by his own admission, it provides him with a "kingdom of his own" over which he has control and in which he can do the things he likes to do. His work on the island is totally fulfilling for him.

Isn't that what many of us are seeking—an island, a *kingdom* where we can be master of our destiny? The island/kingdom may come in different forms for each of us.

To what does Richard credit his successful mid-career change? He says:

> Too many people blame their boss, their wife, (or) their job (for) what is wrong with their lives. In my case, it was my own fault... I was always thinking it was others that were to blame. We don't look at ourselves often enough as the reason for our problems.

When asked what advice he would give someone seeking a mid-career change, he says:

1.   "Know your strengths and your weaknesses. Position yourself in a career so that you emphasize your strengths and minimize your weaknesses. Don't fight upstream all the time. Most people with problems cannot deal with their weaknesses. Don't go mountain climbing if you don't like heights!" This was the most important thing he learned at Harvard.

2.   "Structure your life to fit your interests and talents. Finding your niche is very important. Some of our Fijian workers are more happy (and thus successful) than some of the millionaire guests who visit our island."

3.   "Don't blame others for your problems. Accept responsibility for making a change."

4.   "Don't ever say 'I can't.' It is amazing what you can do if you want to do it badly enough."

5.   "When you are in an environment in which you have no control—get out of it!"

6.   "Realize that neither money, nor escape (through) alcohol, are the answers to insecurities or lack of fulfillment."

He believes the real answer is to find something to do that is worth doing, regardless of the income or shielding effect against insecurity. He concedes that a certain amount of money is necessary, but for Richard, the amount earned is not significant compared to doing something with which he is comfortable and believes is worthwhile.

Richard emphasizes that to truly know yourself in terms of real strengths and preferences, as well as weaknesses, is the key to finding fulfillment. He feels strongly that each individual must assume responsibility for such awareness, and until they do, they are seriously disadvantaged in finding their niche.

Postscript: At the present time, the island and Richard continue to flourish. The island enjoys an international reputation and was chosen as the site of the movie, *The Blue Lagoon*. Richard is still enthusiastic about building the future of the island and its resort as a refuge for both the inhabitants and guests.

Chapter One:

The Employment Picture Today

The crowning fortune of a man is to be born to some pursuit which finds him employment and happiness, whether it be to make baskets, or broadswords, or canals, or statues or songs.
                                        Ralph Waldo Emerson

The Changing Job Market

Change is the order of the day. It was the buzz word of the 1980s, and it is reality in the 1990s. Nowhere is this more true than in the workplace. To some, this may spell disaster; and to others, it can mean opportunity and a renewed life.

What has caused so many mid-career changes? Mergers, downsizing, foreign competition, and technology have made the workplace less stable. Also, increasing entrepreneurial interests, more women in the workplace, the quest for more fulfilling careers, and society's trend toward increased mobility have changed today's employees. These trends have resulted in a reduced sense of loyalty between employers and employees. This, in turn, has brought about more terminations and early retirements, as well as a reduction in the average length of time an employee spends with a given employer.

Computer and other technological changes will replace many middle management personnel. The General Motors, IBM, and Chrysler layoffs of the early 1990s are evidence of this. These people will have to be retrained or make abrupt career changes (sometimes at lower pay) in order to make a living.

High school drop-outs will also bring dramatic problems to society when they find no **niche** to fill in the workplace. This puts greater demands on the welfare system and increases crime, homelessness, and other social problems.

Today's job market has another difference from the job markets of the past. Large and medium sized organizations, once the most likely source of employment, are **downsizing**. People in transition must now consider looking for positions in smaller firms, in the temporary market, or in areas that are very different from the type of job they held. *U.S. News and World Report* (Oct. 26, 1992) quotes a Dun and Bradstreet survey as stating that over 80% of the new jobs to be created in the coming year are to be found in businesses with 100 or less employees.

The administrative and management positions created in small firms often require people with a broad base of skills and experience. This can work to the advantage of the person making a mid-career change, although they may be required to start at a lower compensation level than the one they left.

Furthermore, computer literacy, sales abilities, and entrepreneurial skills are becoming high demand areas in many industries. People with such skills who are willing to begin at lower levels will have a higher chance of securing new employment opportunities.

It is also important to consider that many people making mid-career changes once held positions that were **organization specific** or **occupation specific** knowledge-based jobs. This means that as long as their job requirements remained the same, people with that knowledge or skill could depend upon a job. However, with major changes in the ways in which organizations operate, many job categories and functions have been eliminated. For example, advances in computer technology, robotics, and information exchange and processing have eliminated many jobs that only people with experience in those categories could formerly fill. These people find that although they held significant roles for 20 years, changes in the workplace have created demands for different types of skills than they possess. Now, they must build upon other skills in order to stay competitive.

Additional changes are reflected in personnel shortages in many areas of employment, and in an overabundance of personnel in others. More positions are being created and training programs are expanding. Jobs that have existed for decades have been eliminated and new areas of employment, unheard of in the 1980s, have been created. Larger corporations have cut three and a half million jobs from the payrolls since 1980. Small businesses have generated 20 million new jobs in that same period. In addition, countless changes in the workplace are important factors. The ratio of whites to non-whites, males to females, and young to old has shifted dramatically. More people, especially women, have become **entrepreneurs** during the 1980s. The women's movement has had a tremendous impact on the total job market. Increasing numbers of women have entered non-traditional fields, and the trend is continuing. In 1988, 10,920 women graduated from engineering colleges compared to 878 in 1975.

Matching Jobs To Interests

The United States offers a generally favorable employment market, yet we have a real problem. The labor demand simply does not match today's interests or training.

In 1990 the Gallup Organization conducted a survey of 1,350 people for the National Occupational Information Coordinating Committee. Their findings showed that most American workers do what they do simply because of a lack of choice. Only 41% of those surveyed hold jobs that they had planned to hold. Other findings showed that 18% of the survey participants obtained their current job by chance; 12% took the only job available; and 65% would explore other career options. Nearly one-third of the people surveyed expected to change jobs in the next three years.

Ironically, people have more of a choice than they think. However, they must make the effort to examine the options that are available to them. Much of the problem lies in not understanding what to expect in the job market. Many people do not know what they want from a job, nor do they know how to go about reaching the goals that would fit their interests and needs.

Technological Change

Technology, which often creates new fields, has been a big factor in recent layoffs for employees—especially at the middle management level. General Motors is a classic example of a company that is following this trend. Robots have replaced approximately two-thirds of the assembly line jobs, say Marvin Cetron and Owen Davies, authors of *American Renaissance: Our Life at the Turn of the 21st Century* (New York: St. Martin's Press, 1989). They predict that within the next decade, 250,000 additional robots will replace four million workers. Although new positions will replace these jobs, the new positions will require different skills and training. This will create hardships for many unless the displaced people can be retrained. Those who cannot be retrained will have to accept lower level jobs with less income. In the 1980s this happened to millions of employees who could not or would not be retrained. For those caught in the transition, this results in stress and a reduced standard of living.

Foreign Competition

Foreign competition has put intense pressure on American companies to become more efficient, prompting a substantial reduction in the work force at all levels. This has resulted in short-term layoffs, early retirements, outright terminations, temporary employment and plant relocations. A *mean and lean* mentality has swept into business, industry, government, and education like a virus. Many large U.S. organizations were *fat* in personnel and the change was overdue. However, it has forced millions of blue and white collar workers into mid-career changes that were not anticipated in the early 1980s. Even though American companies have expanded operations abroad, most of the employees in those countries are local nationals with only a few jobs filled by U.S. citizens.

Quality of Life

The quest for a better quality of life is another major factor in the decision to make a mid-career change. Finding the right balance between work and your personal life is very important. Much of life is wrapped up in work. When work is not going well, your personal life often suffers too. Finding a more satisfying and fulfilling career can improve your quality of life. For most people, simply having a job is not enough; they seek a job they can enjoy—even if it means compromising on other

factors such as financial rewards. Henry David Thoreau once said, "The mass of men lead lives of quiet desperation." Nowhere is this more true than in the world of work; but it doesn't have to be this way.

Employee Burn-Out

Increasing numbers of individuals are finding they are **burned-out** or *stressed-out* and they put much of the blame on job related activities. Not only the duties of the job itself, but also the activities associated with their job can lead to burn-out. Child care, household duties, and the underlying stress of perceived and actual neglect of the family build up over time and eventually result in burn-out. Often, conflicting work shifts, transportation, and too many work hours take their toll both physically and mentally. Consultants have made new careers of providing seminars and counseling services for people who are burned-out. Threatened layoffs and forced early retirements are stressful to employees who perceive a constant threat hanging over their heads. All this creates an anxiety in the work force that encourages change.

Departures

Work force reductions have resulted in employee departures for a number of reasons. Employee relocation is one example. Sometimes workers are offered jobs elsewhere with the same company; however the new location often has a jarring impact on the employee and the family. This, alone, can be sufficient to warrant a mid-career change.

Even an employee who has earned a comfortable position over several years is a potential victim of work force reduction. Even if the employee is not terminated, the perks and privileges gradually may be withdrawn. The individual may not be included in meetings he or she would normally attend. He or she may be asked to relocate not once, but twice in a short time. Support staff may be decreased. Signals may be sent that no promotion is imminent. Lateral transfers may be offered. Salaries may level off, or even be reduced. This is a quiet, and sometimes cruel, way of getting an employee to look for greener pastures. Surprisingly, many employees refuse to get the message; or if they do understand what is occurring, they don't do anything about it. They hang on until the end— sometimes with tragic results. Those employees who do face reality and decide to make a mid-career change often wait too long. Sometimes people find they could have made a much better transition from one job to another at an earlier time.

Some people think that to make a change is to admit failure— especially if the change is to a less prestigious or lower paying job. The feeling of failure may persist even though the new job is more comfortable to the individual, his family, and his mental and physical well-being. This is the result of an ego problem, and can lead you to make a wrong decision.

The Career Ladder

Corporate America has always geared its employees to climbing the career ladder. In the past, those who refused to climb were viewed as failures in the eyes of the employer and the employees' peers. Today, however, more people are questioning this standard. "Am I doing the job I want to do?" and "Is a higher position worth the added stress?" For many people, this is a difficult decision to make. People are looking for a comprehensive view of work that relates to their total view of life. They want to bring quality of life to their career.

People who decide to make a change usually do so because they feel they are no longer benefiting from the situation. There is a delicate balance in the employee-employer relationship. When the balance is upset, someone feels cheated. If the employer feels cheated, the employee will often be terminated. If an employee evaluates the overall situation and feels used, he or she is likely to decide to leave the position. More and more people are making mid-career changes after evaluating their current positions and analyzing their goals.

Salaries

Throw out the book when it comes to predicting wages and salaries in the 1990s job market. Some assembly workers who received $15.00 to $20.00 per hour and found their jobs obsolete have been retrained for new jobs near that level of income. Others would not or could not be retrained into jobs of their liking or capabilities, forcing them to accept much lower paying jobs. A lot of people entered service industries that traditionally pay lower wages and benefits. Many in higher level positions, who could transfer to a related industry, did so at a wide range of salaries.

In the 1990s, the opportunities to transfer for workers over age 50 will decrease—mainly because this age group is becoming more available to employers. Most large corporations and government agencies simply do not hire new employees in this age bracket. Despite the claim that they do not **discriminate** because of age, etc., most companies want to promote from within. There are still ample new opportunities for those over 50, but not with the larger organizations. Exceptions to this rule may be colleges and universities who are going to be faced with a great shortage of professors in almost every discipline.

While you are at it, throw out the old rule for calculating salaries of 1,000 times your age. This is not valid today and will not be in the future. For example, college graduates, like other age groups in the total work force, show a vast difference in average earnings in different fields. See Table 1-1. This trend will continue simply because the demand for the technical disciplines is increasing faster than the number of graduates each year.

Bachelor's Degree Graduates

Academic Majors	Estimated Starting Salary
Chemical Engineering	$40,480
Mechanical Engineering	$35,970
Electrical Engineering	$34,982
Computer Science	$34,259
Industrial Engineering	$33,807
Civil Engineering	$30,756
Nursing	$29,572
Chemistry	$29,298
Physics	$29,080
Accounting	$27,849
Mathematics	$27,023
Geology	$27,010
Financial Administration	$25,993
General Business Admin.	$24,978
Personnel Administration	$24,503
Agriculture	$24,358
Marketing/Sales	$24,163
Social Science	$22,162
Telecommunications	$21,721
Communications	$21,604
Retailing	$20,958
Liberal Arts/Arts & Letters	$20,958
Advertising	$20,943
Human Ecology/Home Economics	$20,640
Education	$20,311
Hotel, Rest. Inst. Mgt.	$20,188
Natural Resources	$19,654
Journalism	$19,069

Averages for Graduate Degree Levels

MBA	$37,896
Masters	$35,735
Ph.D.	$40,711

Source: Estimates by John D. Shingleton and L. Patrick Scheetz, Director, Collegiate Employment Research Institute, Michigan State University, using data from the *Salary Survey*, July 1992, published by the College Placement Council, Inc., Bethlehem, PA.

Table 1-1: Estimated Starting Salaries
for New College Graduates of 1993

Longevity

Another factor in the increasing number of job changes is the attitude toward longevity within a single company. Mobility is the name of the game. Years ago, companies thought in terms of lifetime employment for their employees. That has changed dramatically in the last decade. College professors recommend that students change employers, especially in the early years, to move up the success ladder. In fact, five years with one company is considered stable employment. The sophistication of the job seeker is much greater today than in the past. The opportunities are greater. There is no **stigma** in changing jobs often. Many employers hire people today expecting to keep them only a few years, planning to move them out if the employees do not reach a certain level in a given time. Public accounting and law firms have done this for many years and now other employers are doing the same.

Supply/Demand Ratio

When evaluating the job market of tomorrow, it is important to understand the **supply/demand ratio** of various fields. A supply/demand ratio is the number of potential candidates for a given field compared to the employer demand for those employees. Some areas of employment have a higher supply/demand ratio than others. It is not wise to choose a career solely based on the supply/demand ratio, but it certainly should be considered.

The supply/demand ratio changes somewhat from year to year, but the pattern has been approximately the same for the past decade. It should remain fairly close in the next 10 years. Table 1-2 shows the estimated supply and demand for college graduates for the year 1993. It is based on entry level positions and gives an indication of what employers are looking for at the bachelor's degree level.

As you will note, employers seek business and management, computer and information services, engineering, health professionals, mathematics and physics candidates more than candidates in the social sciences, public affairs, psychology, natural resources, foreign languages, and fine and applied arts.

Estimated Supply and Demand
for College Graduates of 1993

LIMITED SUPPLY
Accounting Coll. Teaching
Accounting, Professional
Business Coll. Tchg. (Ph.D.)
Chemistry Teaching
Earth Science Teaching
Electrical Engineering
Engineering College Tchg.
Finance Coll. Teaching
Human Medicine (MD)
Industrial Arts Teaching
Learning Disabilities Tchg. (MS &
   exper.)
Management Science
Materials Science
Mathematics Teaching
Nursing
Operations Research-Mtg. Science
Osteopathic Medicine (DO)
Physics Teaching (BS, MS, Ph.D.)
School Psychologist/Diagnostician
   (Ed.S. or Ph.D.)
School Social Worker (MSW)
Teaching of Emotionally Disturbed

POSSIBLE SHORTAGE
Accounting
Business Education Teaching
Chemical Engineering
Chemistry
Clinical Laboratory Sciences
Computer Science
Computer Science Coll. Tchg.
Data Processing Teaching
Deaf Education Teaching

Distributive Education Tchg.
Driver Education Teaching
Engineering Mechanics
Environmental Engineering (MS, Ph.D.)
Food Science
Food Systems & Economics
   Management
General Science Teaching
Hotel Rest. & Inst. Mgt.
Hotel Rest. & Inst. Mgt. Coll. Tchg.
Labor & Industrial Relations (MLIR)
MLM-Operations
MLM-Transportation/Physical Distribution
Mechanical Engineering
Medical Technology
Nursing Coll. Tchg.
Pharmacy
Physical Science Teaching
Physics (MS, Ph.D.)
Reading Instr. College Teaching
Reading Instr. Teaching (MA)
School Administration (Supt., Prin., etc.)
School Coaching (Basketball,
   football, swimming, wrestling, etc.)
School Counseling (MA & 3 yrs. exper.)
School Librarian
Special Educ. Coll. Tchg.
School Speech Correctionist (MA)
Systems Science
Teaching the Mentally Handicapped
Teaching the Visually Handicapped

Table 1-2: Estimated Supply and Demand for
College Graduates of 1993

NEAR BALANCE
Administration in Higher Education
   (housing, admissions, placement
   financial aid, etc.)
Agribusiness and Nat. Resources
   Education
Agribusiness and Nat. Resources
   Communications
Agricultural Economics
Agricultural Education Teaching
Animal Science
Art Teaching
Arts & Letters College Tchg.
Audiology & Speech Science (MS)
Biochemistry
Biophysics
Botany & Plant Pathology (Ph.D.)
Building Construction
Civil Engineering
Clinical Psychologist (Ph.D.)
Counseling-Agency (MS)
Criminal Justice College Teaching
Crop Science
Dietetics
Economics
English Teaching
Engineering Arts
Financial Administration
Foreign Language (BA, MA, Ph.D.)
   Russian
Forestry
French Teaching
General Business Administration
Home Economics Teaching
Horticulture
Human Ecology/Coll. Teaching
Institutional Administration
Instrumental Music Teaching
Landscape Architecture

Marketing
Mathematics
Merchandising Management
Microbiology & Pub. Health (MS, Ph.D.)
MLM-Purchasing
Packaging
Physics (BS)
Physiology (MS, Ph.D.)
Sanitary Engineering (MS)
Social Work (MSW)
Soil Sciences
Spanish Teaching
Statistics
Teaching English as a Second
   Language (MS)
Teaching the Physically Handicapped
Telecommunications - ITS option
Urban Planning
Veterinary Medicine (DVM)
Vocal Music Teaching
Zoology (MS, Ph.D.)

ADEQUATE SUPPLY
Advertising
Agriculture/Coll. Teaching
Agricultural Engineering
Astronomy
Biological Science
Botany & Plant Pathology (BS, MS)
Child Development
Child Development Tchg.
Clothing & Textiles
Communication Arts Coll. Tchg.
Communication
Counseling Student Per. Serv. Coll. Tchg.
Criminal Justice
Criminalistics
Elementary Education/Coll. Teaching
Elementary Education Teaching

Table 1-2: Estimated Supply and Demand
for College Graduates (cont.)

English
Entomology
Family Ecology
Family Economics & Mgmt.
Family Studies
Fisheries & Wildlife
Foods & Nutrition
Foreign Languages (BA, MA, Ph.D.)
    German & Romance Lang.
Geography
Geology
Geophysics
German Teaching
History (BA)
History Teaching
Home Economics Teaching
Human Nutrition
Humanities
Interior Design
International Relations
Journalism Teaching
Microbiology & Pub. Health (BS)
Multidisciplinary Social Science Teaching
Music Therapy
Natural Science Coll. Tchg.
Nutritional Sciences
Packaging
Parks & Recreation Resources
Personnel Administration (BA, MBA)
Physical Science
Physiology (BS)
Public Administration
Public Affairs Management
Resource Development
Social Science
Social Studies Teaching
Teacher Educ. Coll. Tchg.
Therapeutic Recreation

Travel & Tourism Mgt.
Zoology (BS)

SURPLUS
Anthropology
Art
Biology Tchg.
Conservation Nat. Res. Tchg.
Economics Teaching
Educational Psychology (MS)
Family Community Services
Family & Consumer Resources
Geography Teaching
Government Teaching
Health Education Teaching
Human Ecology (General)
Journalism
Latin Teaching
Linguistics
Philosophy
Physical Education Teaching
Political Science Teaching
Psychology (BS, MA)
Psychology Teaching
Psychology Coll. Teaching
Recreation
Religion
Russian Teaching
Social Science Coll. Tchg.
Social Work (BS)
Sociology
Sociology College Teaching
Sociology Teaching
Speech/Communications Teaching
Theatre
Theatre Teaching

Source: Scheetz, L. Patrick. Director, Collegiate Research Institute, Michigan State University, Collegiate Employment Institute.

Table 1-2: Estimated Supply and Demand
for College Graduates (cont.)

This does not mean there are not opportunities in the surplus areas. However, it does suggest that the supply will be greater than the demand and candidates seeking employment in these areas will probably have to work harder at finding their niche.

Retail jobs are the fastest growing category of service jobs. Their number is expected to grow by three million between now and the end of the century. (Personic, V.A. "Industry Output and Employment: A Slower Trend for the Nineties." *Monthly Labor Review*. U.S. Dept. of Labor, Bureau of Labor Statistics. Volume 112, No. 11 Washington, D.C. Nov. 1989.)

The number of jobs in information services will continue to increase dramatically in the next five years. For example, demand for electronics engineers is expected to increase by 40%, and demand for computer scientists will increase by 50% from the 1980s to the 1990s. The number of mechanics, installers and repair persons for general technology related products will increase by 13% in the same time period. Repair persons for computers will increase 60% (Silvesteri, G., Lukasiewicz, J. "Projections of Occupational Employment, 1988-2000." *Monthly Labor Review*, Nov. 1989.)

The most likely employment paths for individuals affected by downsizing in the 1990s include retraining in technical and information-based careers, re-employment in companies of 50 or under, sales positions, or in international firms. Positions in international firms will continue to grow significantly through the end of the century.

There will be a shortfall of over 500,000 scientists and engineers by the year 2010. For example, state highway work requires an expected 2.5% of civil engineers a year. But the number of college graduates in this field has dropped by 20% since 1985 to fewer than 8,000 a year.

There is no substitute for being among the best in any field.
Those falling in that category will always find a demand for
their services. There is one exception, however. If you are
over 50 years of age, some large companies may still overlook
your talents in favor of someone who is younger.

Age Discrimination

There is no question that age discrimination exists in some
organizations. Elderly people have been especially hard hit
in recent years as employers seek ways to downsize and
cut costs. Older employees are often the first to be let go.
Furthermore, they face another problem when seeking new
employment because some employers are reluctant to hire
older workers. Some employers think that older employers
add to the cost of medical benefits.

"Employees once revered as reservoirs of wisdom are now
viewed as symbols of decay and death," says Jack Levin,
Professor of Sociology at Northeastern University, and author
of *Ageism: Prejudice and Discrimination Against the Elderly*
(Belmont CA: Wadsworth Publishing Co., 1980). He further
states, "There's a widespread stereotype that goes back
decades, even centuries, according to which older people
are stupid, incompetent, unproductive and can't learn."

Individuals who are caught in these circumstances must
recognize these obstacles when seeking new employment.
They must convince employers that older employees are not
past their prime and have a great deal to offer. Here is where
selling becomes a major part of the job hunt. More on this
follows in Chapter Eight: Marketing Your Talents.

Demographics

The quality of the work force, in terms of years of education, is increasing in percentage. Demographers estimate that about three-fourths of the students currently in high school will graduate, and about 45% of those will enter college. Twenty-one percent of those who enter college will earn bachelor's degrees. During 1992 more bachelors degrees were awarded by our colleges and universities than ever before. See Figure 1-1. This increase will continue well into the 1990s. The number of master's degree graduates and doctoral degree graduates also have increased significantly. See Figures 1-2 and 1-3.

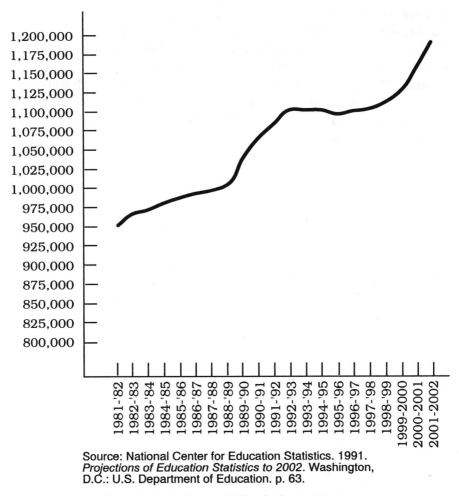

Source: National Center for Education Statistics. 1991.
Projections of Education Statistics to 2002. Washington,
D.C.: U.S. Department of Education. p. 63.

Figure 1-1: Earned Bachelor's Degrees
in the United States, Conferred and Projected

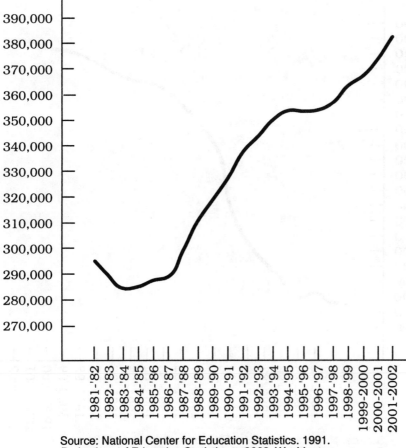

Source: National Center for Education Statistics. 1991.
Projections of Education Statistics to 2002. Washington,
D.C.: U.S. Department of Education. p. 64.

Figure 1-2: Earned Master's Degrees
in the United States, Conferred and Projected

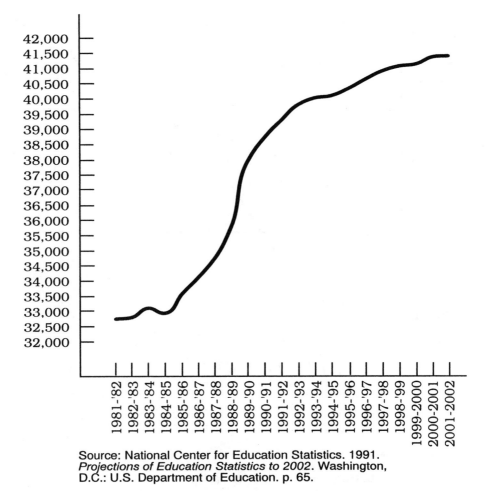

Source: National Center for Education Statistics. 1991.
Projections of Education Statistics to 2002. Washington,
D.C.: U.S. Department of Education. p. 65.

Figure 1-3: Earned Doctorate's Degrees
in the United States, Conferred and Projected.

In 1979, 46% of the college graduates were males. In 1986, the number dropped to only 38%. This means that more women entered the work force with degrees during those years.

The United States needs about 8% of its 22 year-olds to go into science and engineering to meet the needs of business, industry, government and education. Currently, only 7% are going into the sciences and engineering. Over the years, this will create a substantial shortfall of people in these areas. There has been a shortage of engineering professors for several years; this will become more acute in the 1990s.

Another point to recognize is that the **global economy** is here. There are enormous markets outside the United States that will significantly impact jobs in this country.

Second, value systems are changing; and the work environment must also change to accommodate the worker.

Third, more small companies will emerge and large companies will reduce in size. Companies will continue to move from cities to the suburbs.

Fourth, it will become harder to produce enough money to pay for the increasing number of retirees.

Fifth, emphasis on education at the elementary and secondary levels will become increasingly important as society faces the problem of increasing numbers of dropouts.

These factors will result in some substantial, sometimes devastating, changes. It behooves all those examining their careers and contemplating change to realize mid-career change can happen for a variety of reasons over which you have little or no control. It then becomes important that you:

1.   Understand what is going on around you. Analyze where you fit into the scheme of things.

2.   Prepare and be flexible. Recognize that you must be able to adjust to different conditions and different ways of doing things.

3.   Don't be too rigid in what you will accept if faced with alternatives.

4.   Stay current in your line of work. Keep up-to-date on the latest innovations and technology. Keep track of employers and contacts in your field of work in case a change is imminent.

5.   Be alert to signs of **deterioration** in your employment areas. Usually there are strong indicators before drastic action is taken (i.e., foreign competition is taking over the company, plants in your industry are closing, employer is losing money). It is amazing how many people ignore signs of this nature until the last minute.

6.   Recognize that a job that is stable today can turn into a high risk category very quickly.

7.   Expect the unexpected.

Is More Education The Answer?

One of the questions asked by those suddenly facing a mid-career change is, "Should I take time off now to go back to college and get an MBA or some other degree?" This, of course, depends upon your area of specialization, your financial status, your family, etc. Generally, however, acquiring a master's or doctoral degree on a full-time basis is a marginal economic investment. Two to five years with no income— plus tuition and living expenses—is a lot of income to attempt to recover for anyone over forty. It is much wiser to get advanced degrees in the early years after earning a bachelor's degree. Or, obtain a bachelor's degree and then earn the advanced degree by attending school part-time while working. Financially, this is by far the best deal—even though it takes longer to obtain the degree.

There is no question that advanced degrees can enhance long-range incomes and, in some cases, are a must for entry into a given field. But for mid-career changes, experience, knowledge, and planning skills far exceed any benefits an advanced degree can give you. It is not a good idea to pursue an MBA or any other advanced degree simply to have it on your resume.

Attending seminars, workshops, and conferences to acquire new marketable skills is a good way to get good solid career help economically and quickly. However, it is best to do this while you are still employed, rather than attending such programs after you have ended your employment. This approach can save you both time and money.

Regional Differences

The area in which you live will affect your employment opportunities. It is important to consider your chances for finding opportunity in a given area before moving there, changing your career direction, or pursuing education or retraining.

The northeastern states hold greater competition for most jobs than many other regions simply because of the concentration of people. Furthermore, this region is dominated by many of the older industries that currently reflect a surplus of job applicants. However, the Northeast still demonstrates some moderate demand for skilled personnel in high-tech industries related to health care services and products, including the pharmaceutical industry and its vendors. There are also opportunities in many small entrepreneurial start-up firms with five or less employees.

A look at the midwestern states shows that the strongest industries include temporary agencies and services, health care services (both research and primary care), and related fields such as medical technology and insurance. Also, as in most other regions, the recreation industry offers opportunity with both large and small employers.

The Southwest also shows good demand in the recreation industries and in most young or new industries such as high-tech and business services. However, as with most other regions, job seekers will need to be skilled or willing to work in small start-up businesses. Opportunity is expected to be slow but steady in this region as population gradually shifts in this direction.

The Southeast has been particularly hard hit by the recession of the early 1990s. But, as with the other regions, there is still a demand for people with sales and marketing abilities. Of course, what this means is that only those people with the greatest skills in this area will find employment. Also, as in other regions, much of the business growth and opportunity will be in smaller businesses.

The Northwest has also had a cutback in job opportunities in the larger organizations. Small businesses are showing greater growth as more experienced people are leaving the larger employers to become consultants, contract employees, and part-time workers.

The important thing to recognize in your job hunt is that the employment demand is different from region to region. The secret is to identify those differences and increase your chances for employment by focusing on those areas with the greatest potential.

Requirements For A Successful Mid-Career Change

Certain elements are necessary for a successful career change. These will be addressed in more detail later; but for now, here is a short list to keep in mind as you pursue your goal.

1. Most job hunters do not spend enough time on the job hunt. They wait for things to happen rather than making things happen. If you really want to make a job change, plan on spending 15 to 30 hours a week solely on your job search.

2. Working job hunters usually visit two or three employers a month. That is not enough to produce results. Quadruple that figure and you will begin seeing results. Unemployed job seekers should see two to three employers per day.

3. *You* are responsible for finding a job—not a friend or a relative or a counselor. Accept the responsibility and act.

4. Be **aggressive**.

5. Use all the resources available to you:

    a. advertisements
    b. trade journals
    c. conventions
    d. personal contacts
    e. resumes
    f. direct application
    g. placement offices
    h. private agencies
    i. government agencies
    j. self-employment

6. Don't be discouraged if you are rejected. Keep a positive outlook.

7. Be persistent.

Mid-Career Changes for People With Disabilities

People with disabilities should use most of the same techniques and resources for finding a job as others. Depending upon the disability, a special effort should be made to make personal contact with the people doing the hiring. Here, salesmanship plays a major role in convincing the employer that you can do the job. Sometimes it may be necessary to accept a position where you are **underemployed** to prove yourself. This also applies to people who do not have disabilities. In some cases, it is advisable to accept a part-time or temporary position to demonstrate you can perform in a given job. Don't be afraid to accept such jobs. Other opportunities often open up once you demonstrate what you can do and how well you perform. The biggest problem is getting into the work environment.

One of the best sources of career planning and job hunting is the National Library Service for the Blind and Physically Handicapped, Library of Congress, 1291 Taylor Street, N.W., Washington, D.C. 20542. Many books are available on tape for the visually impaired. They will send these to you free of charge with appropriate playback equipment. Remember, every job seeker has some disadvantages when seeking a job. The secret is to identify those jobs where the disadvantages are of little or no importance in performing the job.

Going Into Business For Yourself

Self-employment is of special interest to many people who want to make a career change. This may include purchasing a franchise or an existing business, start-up opportunities, etc. These are good options for some people. Although the past has shown that many new businesses fail within the first three years, recent figures indicate a rise in the success of start-up businesses in recent years. The following table shows what new business owners say about themselves.

New-Business Profile

Based on a survey of 2,994 new companies

How old were you when you became owner or principal manager of your present business?

20-29 years	26%
30-39 years	39
40-49 years	24
50 or more	11

How did you become owner or principal manager of your present business?

Started it	64%
Purchased it (Not from family)	30
Inherited it	2
Promoted to ownership	1
Brought into ownership	2

How large do you expect your gross sales to be in two years?
(In thousands of dollars)

$50-99	14%
$100-199	22
$200-349	16
$350-499	6
$500-749	7
$750-999	3
$1,000-2,999	8
$3,000 and over	3

Does your firm operate under a franchise name, e.g., McDonald's?

Yes	11%
No	87
N.A.	2

Source: Roger Ricklefs, "Road to Success Becomes Less Littered With Failures," *The Wall Street Journal*, October 10, 1989. Reprinted by permission of *The Wall Street Journal* © 1989 Dow Jones & Company, Inc. All Rights Reserved Worldwide.

Table 1-3: New-Business Profile

The study, commissioned by the American Express Company and the National Federation of Independent Business, explored the reasons some companies survived. The survey included 2,994 new businesses and was conducted by Arnold C. Cooper, William C. Dunklegerb and Carolyn Y. Woo. Here are some of their findings:

1. Initial financial backing was very important to success. Eighty-four percent of those who had $50,000 initially survived. Of those who had less than $20,000, only 74% survived.

2. Successful entrepreneurs generally spend more of their time either selling or working with customers than doing any other business related activity.

3. Companies with outside investors were more likely than others to show signs of growth.

4. Owners were likely to be "acting on a business idea that occurred in a previous job." They also tended to have more formal education.

5. Fifty-four percent said that government regulation was worse than originally feared, while 19% said it wasn't as bad as expected.

6. Seventy-seven percent of the new businesses surveyed survived three years or more.
(Roger Ricklefs, "Road to Success Becomes Less Littered With Failures," *The Wall Street Journal*, October 10, 1989.)

Finally, remember that research on career opportunities, whether focusing on a major change in direction or a simple change of job, requires many considerations. These include finances, career growth, and security as well as geographical preference, cost of living, life style, and the interests of your family. The earlier you consider these important factors in your research, the more likely you are to move in the direction of your ultimate goal: more career and personal growth and satisfaction.

From a Homemaker to a Business Woman

The number of women entering the job market is growing at an increasing rate; employers can no longer refuse to hire a woman if she has the proper qualifications for a given vacancy. Still, many women feel employers have a long way to go before women are treated fairly in the business world. This is true in many cases, but for job-seeking purposes it is best to assume there is an equal opportunity. Don't enter an interview situation with a chip on your shoulder.

Homemakers choosing to enter or re-enter the business world after the childrearing days are over will find it is not an easy path. To begin with, younger is better in the eyes of most employers, especially if you are looking at middle and top level positions. Employers may say, "When we hire someone at age forty-five, and then train her, we don't have many years before she retires."

Certain kinds of work, of course, lend to employment at the middle management level. If the candidate's experience and training are in selling, accounting, retailing, office supervision, computer management, and general administration, then a middle management position is a possibility.

In spite of the negatives that can be presented, there are many positives. One of the best avenues to follow in making the transition from a homemaker to a business person is to begin with part-time work. This provides an opportunity to break into the work force gradually. You can brush up on a few of the latest techniques in surviving in the business world. Best of all, you get the opportunity to show what you can do. Then as new openings occur, you are there to be considered.

An alternative to working part-time is applying for one job as a team. Two women once came to me as a team to apply for a position. I hadn't planned, or even thought, to fill the job that way; but they explained how it would work. It enabled them to carry out their respective responsibilities both at the office and at home. They sold the idea to me and it worked out beautifully. They communicated perfectly (which contributed greatly to their success) and as time went by, they presented programs to others on how jobs can be shared.

Women who have not had paid employment for an extended period of time often choose to return to college for a degree. They hope to re-enter their careers above the clerical or secretarial levels. This is a big gamble for many. When considering this approach, be sure to study the supply/demand ratio in the field you expect to enter. Carefully weigh the cost against the added income you might expect. Many who have pursued additional education have not been satisfied with the results; these people might have been better off entering the job market with their original credentials. Personal gratification, however, is hard to measure, and some people feel better about themselves when they obtain that additional degree.

Many successful women have started their own business after being a homemaker. This has many advantages in that it offers considerable responsibility without having to deal with the corporate ladder of the larger organizations. Self-employment can be risky, but can be a lot of fun for the right person.

Contract Employment

Another possible solution for those seeking mid-career changes is **contract employment**. Under this arrangement, people seeking temporary or part-time employment can find niches in the job market that might not be available through the usual permanent employer. Retired people, especially, may find contract employment a feasible form of work. Ninety percent of all U.S. companies rely on temporary employees at least once a year, spending approximately $49 billion annually. Increasing government regulation regarding selection, promotion, benefits, termination, and related employment issues have made the use of contract employees much more attractive for American industries. *This trend is increasing with no sign of reversing in the near future.* Even the IRS is adding fuel to the fire. They are requiring companies to police their own health and welfare benefits for full-time, regular employees with a complicated maze of new rules, options, exclusions and paperwork. Furthermore, skill shortages in many occupational areas have made it more difficult for some employers to recruit full-time, permanent employees in many technical, support, and professional categories. The result is an increase in the use of contract employees.

Contract employees are used to perform activities or services that do not require regular or permanent staff. They usually work on an hourly or daily basis, and are paid at intervals during the length of the contract. No vacation, retirement, or related benefits are normally included in the contract. In addition, since these are not permanent employees, they are not subject to most policies regarding overtime, promotions, appraisals, etc. There are many obvious advantages to the use of contract employees, not the least of which is cost. Many employers pay 30% or more above the base salary in benefits to permanent employees, not to mention significant recruitment, hiring, and training expenditures.

Another important issue is performance. Permanent employees can maintain moderate or even marginal performance standards and continue employment much more easily than contract employees. If a contract employee does not perform well, termination is usually immediate, and fairly simple. Contract employees can be used to meet temporary demand cycles for products and services that fluctuate seasonally. In addition, businesses do not have to pay unemployment benefits to a contract employee who has been terminated.

Contract employees benefit from the flexibility as well. While they do not have the security of a regular position, they do have the option of working at times that fit their needs. Also, they can leave work they do not like without it affecting their work record. Contract employees can avoid many of the frustrations of regular employment such as internal politics, disagreeable supervisors, and involuntary relocations. Most important to many though, is the fact that there is an increasing demand for contract employees. This is where many mid-level jobs may be found.

There are two general approaches to contract employment. One is through businesses or agencies that place people with clients and then charge the client for the contract employee. An example would be firms that supply *temporaries*. This type of firm acts as an intermediary between the employee and the employer, and pays the contract employee. Once, most temporaries were in office support areas such as secretaries, receptionists and clerical employees. This business has grown to include employees for almost any kind of employment including accounting, data processing, engineering, sales and other highly specialized skill areas. You may find these agencies by consulting the yellow pages in a telephone directory, referencing professional associations, or investigating business directory sources available in public libraries.

The other approach to contract employment is by direct association with the employer. Here, the potential employee **negotiates** or establishes an individual agreement with the organization. These agreements generally are based upon an hourly or daily rate to be paid as long as the contract employee works. Because the use of contract employees is becoming more common, organizations usually have guidelines for paying such employees.

Many companies use retirees as contract employees. In such cases, the employer may simply arrange to pay the employee their former hourly rate, minus the benefits, for the number of hours worked each week. Of course, if the employee normally receives retirement benefits, the employer continues to pay them.

Another option is a fixed sum contract for a particular job regardless of the number of hours expended. Finding direct contract employment is best achieved by using the networking procedure described in Chapter Eight, or inquiring at organizations who use contract employees in your skill area. If you do not require the security of a permanent position, this may be an excellent option to consider. In any case, it may be a useful short-term option while searching for a more ideal position.

Hiring a Career Counselor

Finding a true professional who will provide sincere advice and positive results at a reasonable fee is not easy, and requires a lot of research on your part. Do preliminary research to identify counselors who might help you by checking the various agencies and professionals in your area. Then, talk to them personally to determine their experience, credentials and level of sincerity. You also should talk to some of their clients before making any commitments, and refrain from making any payments in advance. Obviously, the fee they charge for their services will help you decide.

To find counselors, start with recommendations from your personal contacts, friends, relatives, personnel, etc. Check your local yellow pages and the list of sources in Appendix F.

Questions for Review

1. Why do people think they have little choice in selecting a new career?

2. On which segment of the employment market is the computer creating the most impact?

3. How important is one's quality of life, and how can it affect career decisions?

4. What are some of the signals an employer may send that might indicate an impending reduction in the work force?

5. What is the supply/demand ratio in your chosen career path?

6. Are starting salaries increasing or decreasing for new college graduates?

7. Is more education the answer to your mid-career change?

8. What resources are available to you in your mid-career change?

9. What is one of the best avenues to follow in making the transition from homemaker to business person?

10. What is contract employment?

Chapter Two:
Looking for Self-Fulfillment in Your Career

The workers are the saviors of society, the redeemers of the race.
                              Eugene V. Debs

The Importance of Work

Anyone considering a mid-career change or embarking on a career should understand the importance of work in the pursuit of happiness. Much of the growth and development of this nation is based on the work ethic, yet we seldom acknowledge its importance in our lives until we are without it.

For some, work has a negative meaning. For example, the *American Heritage Dictionary of the English Language* lists the synonyms for work as *labor, toil, drudgery* and *travail*—all negative terms.

Americans seem to have a love/hate attitude toward work. We desire it and worship it, yet we despise it. We believe in work, yet we try to avoid it. We encourage our children to have paper routes, mow lawns and sell lemonade, while we search constantly for labor-saving devices. The negative feelings often are related to the fact that it can be difficult to find the right **niche** in which to work. The secret is to find that correct niche. Once the right niche is found, the attitude toward work becomes positive. Finding the right niche is an essential ingredient in making a mid-career change.

It pays to have a positive attitude toward work. Life in America revolves around one's job. Being unemployed in our society can be very distressing. Furthermore, it is in the world of work where a person will probably make his or her greatest contribution—to himself or herself and to society.

Most of us spend about one-fourth of our lives working. That, alone, is important enough to give it the highest priority in planning our lives. Spending a quarter of our lives doing something we do not enjoy is unthinkable! George Burns showed his understanding of this concept at age 93 when he said, "The reason I'm so old is that I love my work, money is not the answer at all—I just love my work."

We need work, most of us cannot do without it. Those who ignore it pay a pitiful price. Many of the great problems of our society are the result of people who cannot or will not find jobs. The price society pays for unemployment is beyond comprehension.

Recognizing these factors raises the importance of mid-career change to the level it deserves. One of the biggest pitfalls of making a change is the failure to plan for it. Foresight can make your change successful.

Why is finding the right niche in the job market so important? First, it gives us identity. It tells others what we do, and to a large degree, who we are. Many of our surnames are derived from occupations our forefathers had centuries ago. Often, when being introduced to others, our occupation follows our name.

Second, it provides us with the economic means to live and to provide for ourselves and our families. What we do and how well we do it makes a difference in our standard of living. It determines not only how our basic needs (food and shelter) will be met, but the extent to which we will enjoy luxuries and our **leisure** time.

Third, work affects our health. The kind of work we do can effect our general health, causing serious health problems when we are in the wrong job. Unemployment, especially to those continuously employed in the past, can have devastating effects on a person's mental and overall well-being. On the other hand, those in jobs they enjoy and find fulfilling often experience robust health and good spirits, affecting not only themselves but those around them.

Fourth, work is one of the major differences between man and animal. To work is to grow and achieve; and achievement leads to development. Therefore, the development of mankind, in no small measure, is due to work.

Fifth, lack of work results in boredom for those who are energetic and ambitious. There comes a time in most people's lives when it is time to call it quits or at least reduce our pace in the workplace. This is normal as we grow older. Most of us, however, have to have something to do that fills the time we have on earth. Work has proven to be one of the better ways to do this. To be totally without something to do can be a fate worse than death.

Sixth, work is a measuring stick for our abilities and accomplishments. Others measure us by what we do in the world of work. It challenges us to bigger and greater things. It inspires competition among us and tells us who the winners and losers are. We judge ourselves by what we do in the world of work. Furthermore, our work is a major means by which others judge us as well.

Seventh, work provides us with a social network which, when we are in the right niche, enhances our quality of life. We find ourselves dealing with people of similar interests, likes and dislikes, environments, social status, intellect, hobbies, etc. Often, work also provides us with our leisure-time associates, and gives us a network of friends from which to expand.

Finally, work fulfills us. It establishes our place in society. Life without work is life without function. Through work, we serve.

So, a positive attitude toward work will enhance your life. However, you must also find the kind of work that best suits who you are. Find the right niche and all the advantages of work are yours; find the wrong niche and you face continual problems and frustrations.

There is no doubt that as society has evolved, certain kinds of work have made robots out of human beings. Even in the early stages of the industrial revolution when working conditions were at their worst, people gradually improved their status, mainly through economic means. Today, few of those robot jobs exist. Employers and employees have negotiated vacations, more reasonable work hours, and other benefits to improve the economic and social status of workers. Most are now able to pursue outside interests as well.

The proper combination of work and leisure requires a constant give and take of **priorities**, and is more of an art than a science. Those whose ultimate goal of work is to provide a lifetime of leisure will find they are pursuing a false objective. A life of leisure is a make-believe goal that merely destroys all the good that work can offer.

In the later years, a more likely objective is one that provides opportunity to do what you would most like to do when you want to do it. Thus, work that is flexible and allows for leisure time while providing challenge is the best of all worlds. There is tremendous freedom of choice in this country. Make the most of it.

Defining Real Career Success

Being able to define career success in your own terms is important when making a mid-career change. In fact, it is a critical step toward building a solid career. You have to know what you are looking for if you are going to find it. Too many people drift with the current, letting chance or fate take them down their career path. This works for some people, but it is not the route to take if you are trying to get the percentages in your favor.

Success in life involves more than being successful financially. Yet, too often in our society, that is the measuring stick of success. For most of us, one of the principle motivations for working is money. Therefore, financial gains cannot be ignored when determining success for most people.

True success is much more than financial gain. We also work for the enjoyment and satisfaction it brings, the social contacts it generates, and the opportunities that unfold. It often fills the need to create, develop and implement plans by which we can be measured. It offers us **prestige** and **status**.

Journalist Leo Rosten put it quite well, "The purpose of life is to matter, to count, to stand for something, to have it make a difference that we lived at all." That is what it is all about. If your goal is to be a success in life, chances are it includes the desire to make a lasting impression in some way.

The Measuring Stick of Success

We have listed some of the ingredients for success; but, how do you measure success? Is success based upon finding an identity with which we are comfortable? In order to be successful, shouldn't that identity continue to provide

satisfaction and interest in your life? Dr. Victor E. Frankl, a
well-known psychiatrist and author, made an interesting
observation:

> It is my conviction that man should not, indeed,
> cannot, struggle for identity in a direct way; rather
> he finds identity to the extent to which he commits
> himself to something beyond himself, to a cause
> greater than himself.

A successful person, then, lives for a commitment beyond
himself or herself. Some people measure their success
through the happiness, fulfillment, and respect of their family.
They measure their success by how they meet their **obligations** to others in the family by living and working in a way
that is respectable, honest and responsible.

We all have different measuring sticks for a successful career.
Promotions help many of us measure our
success; but beware of promotions that
can have an adverse effect
on your life
and your
family's well-
being. Work
becomes a
problem when
it interferes
with home life
or threatens
your health.
While it is necessary
to focus on skills and career advancement,
most people find that the important things in life revolve
around their family and career. They are dependent upon one
another. Separating one from the other leaves a void that
conflicts with the true meaning of success.

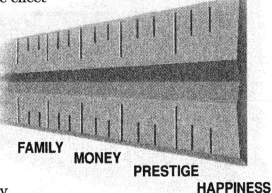
FAMILY   MONEY   PRESTIGE   HAPPINESS

Decide what *you* want out of a career rather than what you feel others think is a successful career. To be truly successful in your career, it is important to realize the difference between the concept of progress and one's personal success. Many people think they know what success is only to learn later how wrong they were.

Plateauing On The Job

One of the major reasons people seek mid-career change is that they feel they have plateaued in their job—they no longer find it a challenge. They feel that they can no longer grow in their position and that they must spend the rest of their days repeating what they are now doing. This can damage one's ego as well as their motivation to do a better job. Reaching a **plateau** in your job can be frustrating and stressful. Some people describe it as feeling as if they have been put on the scrap pile of life.

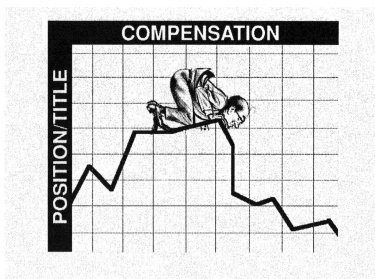

This is a time to look for other **objectives** and **goals**—a time for reassessment of where you are and where you want to go. But before you do that, recognize that everyone reaches a plateau somewhere in their career. Even when you get to the top of your organization, there is a plateau. The fact is, there is too much emphasis placed on moving up the organizational ladder. **Plateauing** can have its advantages if your attitude is right. Accept the fact that plateauing is inevitable; accepting it results in less stress. Having the wrong attitude toward your leveling off in responsibilities will make you frustrated and discontented.

If you like other factors in your job (pay, benefits, type of work, associates, etc.), you may want to consider remaining at your current level and making the most of it. Of course, not every-body can do this. Yet, millions of people have accepted the reality that they will remain at their current level of employ-ment for a long time. They live a comfortable and happy life. There is nothing wrong with it, in spite of what the MBA schools teach and the success stories of those moving up the ladder. The secret lies in believing in yourself and in your satisfaction with what is happening. The difficult part is overcoming the outside pressures that tell you that you must have a bigger title or more money.

Today, more employees who find themselves on a career plateau are accepting it. They realize that they don't have to keep moving up the ladder to be successful. These people accept the conditions that exist, and rely more on their per-sonal thinking than on what others expect of them. They refuse to be promoted to a level of dissatisfaction—a principle too often ignored by unhappy individuals who call themselves *successful*. Plateauing is not all bad.

Leveling off in a career is not new. Many professional careers plateau at an early stage in terms of prestige, title, perks, etc. Doctors, lawyers, dentists, government workers, teachers, and secretaries plateau and live happy, fulfilled lives. In the corporate structure, however, it takes a certain mental outlook to accept this. Very often it takes more courage to turn down a job with more money, more perks, more prestige, than to accept it—even if the job means less desirable financial rewards.

Plateauing will become much more common and acceptable in the 1990s than in earlier years. It is forecast that the job market of 1995 will have 30 people competing for each available middle management position. This prediction has been made by Ron Zenke, President of Performance Research Associates in Minneapolis. If this is true, more plateauing is inevitable in the future.

If you cannot accept remaining in your current position and you feel overly frustrated, it is time to change something. One of the best ways to do this is to look elsewhere for employment. Changing employers does not necessarily mean you will be in a better world, but it does open up new avenues for potential improvement. The change can be invigorating and challenging. You meet a different group of people in a different environment. All of this can be stimulating. It may even motivate you to do a better job.

Once you have decided upon a change, do something about it. The work force is filled with people who desperately want to make a change but are reluctant to take the necessary steps.

If you feel trapped in your job, or seek a job change for some other reason, this book is written for you. However, it cannot solve your problem unless you feel a total commitment to making a change. You also must be willing to set aside the time, make the effort, and resolve to make a change.

For many, making a mid-career change is not that difficult because they have the **credentials**, the desire and the persistence to bring about a change. Others, however, never get around to making a change simply because they find excuses to avoid the hard decisions that have to be made. There are plenty of excuses for delaying a career change. Once you sense an excuse developing, recognize it for what it is, and take positive steps to avoid it. Don't let **procrastination** prevent you from making a change!

Questions for Review

1. Other than income, what are some reasons for finding the right niche in the job market?

2. What does success mean to you?

3. What does it mean to *plateau* on a job?

4. What is one of the biggest obstacles to overcome when seeking a job change?

5. Do you know anyone who has been promoted to their level of dissatisfaction? If so, why did this happen?

Chapter Three:

When to Leave Your Old Job

He that is afraid to shake the dice will never throw a six.

Old Chinese proverb

Do You Want to Change Jobs?

Saying good-bye to your old job is not easy, particularly if you have held the position for a long time. Before making a job change, look objectively at your reasons for making the change. You may be better off staying where you are. Here are a few factors you should consider before you make your decision:

1. *Skills.* Are you using your training and education? Is the job challenging and mentally stimulating? Do you enjoy what you are doing?

2. *Associates.* Do you enjoy the people with whom you are working? Do they help make your life more enjoyable and interesting?

3. *Environment.* Is the physical setting of your work place healthy? Do you enjoy being there?

4. *Salary.* Is your salary appropriate for your contribution to the organization? Are you making enough money to support your life-style?

5. *Benefits.* Do your insurance and retirement plans meet your needs? Are the vacation, sick leave and overtime benefits competitive?

6. *Hours.* Are your working hours reasonable?

7. *Community.* Is the school system where you live adequate? Are there adequate recreational and cultural programs available?

8. *Family.* Are you able to see your family and relatives with the frequency you desire?

9. *Prestige.* Do you receive the respect of your peers that you need or feel should come with the job? Does management give you the proper recognition?

10. *Supervision.* Is your supervisor responsive to your interests? Are you comfortable with the organizational structure?

11. *Potential.* Does your employer provide the potential for growth and opportunity that you seek?

12. *Company Financial Status.* Is the company going to be around for awhile?

13. *Self-improvement.* Does your employer provide opportunities for additional training?

14. *Geographic Location.* Is the location of your work geographically desirable?

15. *Job Stability.* Have you received any hints of future lay-offs?

Leaving your present position is a big step. Of course, if your job is secure, the decision is completely yours. This is the best position in which to be; you can stay at your present job until you locate the right career opportunity. However, sometimes situations beyond your control may force you into making a change.

WHEN LEAVING IS YOUR DECISION

Analyze Your Reasons For Considering a Job Change

Changing jobs requires a good deal of thought and **analysis**. As mentioned earlier, not all job changes are for the better. While people change jobs, their reasons for doing so are not always well thought out. Considering the items on the previous list can help you avoid the pitfalls many others have encountered. Recognize that all jobs have their shortcomings and everyone, at one time or another, has to do tasks they do not enjoy.

Focusing on one negative factor can become an obsession to the point where you forget all the good elements of a job. In cases like this, try to correct the one undesirable element before considering a job change. Many people have changed jobs only to find themselves worse off than before the change.

REASONS FOR LEAVING
No opportunities for advancement
Future of company looks shaky

REASONS FOR STAYING
Nice place to work
Close to home
Satisfying work
Comfortable

Consider all your options before making the decision to change companies. These options should include the following:

1. Discussions with your boss or co-workers to correct what you consider an unsatisfactory situation.

2. Seek transfers within the company to correct a problem in your immediate work group. This way, you maintain your seniority benefits and location, and you save yourself the mental stress of adjusting to a completely new environment. Do not overlook lateral transfers.

3. Analyze whether patience and time will correct the problem. A change in supervisory personnel can make a tremendous difference in a work situation. If such a change is imminent, a little patience may pay off.

4. Make sure that a solution to your problem is not forthcoming before you make the change.

Identify Your Priorities

In discussing mid-career changes, people often put too much emphasis on finances. When money is the sole issue, needs that add to the individual's satisfaction with work and/or life are often neglected. There are other factors that should be considered as well. The person contemplating a mid-career change should look at all factors, paying particular attention to his or her priorities. This is one of the basic principles of making a successful mid-career transition. Those making unsuccessful changes do so because they failed to look at the whole picture. People who do this are apt to continue in the same rut when they change jobs. They often fail to examine all the aspects of their new prospects.

Career Change Within the Organization

It is important to remember that career change does not always have to mean leaving the organization with which you are currently employed. The grass may appear greener elsewhere because of some small, though significant, problem in your current position. If the problem can be traced to a shortcoming on your part, objective self-assessment may help diagnose and fill this need. If left unaddressed, the problem will continue to exist and may make life even more difficult in another place of employment. Or, perhaps the problem is due to circumstances related to your position, your supervisor, or co-workers. Again, challenges such as these do not necessarily require departure from the organization. Remember to consider practical solutions to your problem within the organization before taking the major step of leaving the company.

WHEN LEAVING IS BEYOND YOUR CONTROL

Trends

Sometimes you have to say good-bye to a job that you do not want to leave. Dramatic changes in the workplace are resulting in a reshuffling of workers. Ironically, a **skill gap** is emerging that can have serious consequences for the business community. Certain positions are increasingly difficult to fill. The cost of living in some areas is outpacing the salaries that companies can afford to offer, forcing many workers to seek other employment. This is complicated by the fact that many new graduates are not prepared for the needs of modern, private enterprise.

Part of the problem is that many older workers will be declared obsolete in their current jobs. Unless they can be retrained for the demands of the new job market, they will be on the streets or accepting jobs at a much lower salary level.

Already there is a desperate need for people to do low-skill jobs. There are enough people to do the work, but many are unwilling to accept the jobs that are available to them.

"The potentially devastating mismatch between workers and (required) skills is emerging from a complex mixture of demographic, technological and social changes," says Robert Boyd of the *Detroit Free Press*. "The number of people, age 20 to 29, will decline from 41 million in 1980 to 34 million in 2000. Census Bureau figures show their share of the population will narrow from 18 to 13 percent." See Table 3-1. These conditions will enhance the employability of older workers, providing they have the motivation and are prepared to retrain for the new jobs that will be available. In many cases, it will also be necessary to take a cut in pay.

Technological changes are also having a dramatic effect on certain segments of the employment market. For example, technological changes in the area of data processing have had a devastating effect on middle management personnel. These changes have affected people in accounting, banking, investment planning, design, **materials logistics**, purchasing, communications, information systems, and research to name a few. While the technological changes have created some jobs, the net result has been a reduction in the total number of jobs.

How the Age of the Workers in the United States is Changing

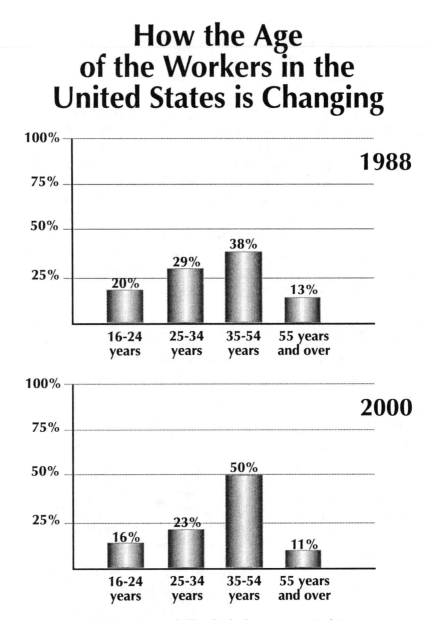

SOURCE: Congressional Office of Technology Assessment, Rand Corp.;
Adapted from Judy Treible/Knight-Ridder Tribune News, Detroit Free Press (May 7, 1989).

Table 3-1: The Age of Workers in the United States

Jobs requiring manual labor have been reduced too. Carpenters, machinists, production workers, and others have encountered very difficult times.

Entry level jobs for college graduates have also been on the down-swing. Opportunities for graduates in the non-technical areas are at the lowest level since the early 1980s.

The social changes brought about by this mismatch between skills and workers are also becoming more and more evident. Employees forced into a mid-career change often have to relocate to a different area of the country. The Northeast, for example, which had low unemployment rates in the early 1980s now has one of the highest unemployment rates. This has forced many employees and their families to either relocate or change their life-styles drastically.

When terminated, some employees are left without adequate health benefits. The sudden loss of health insurance can create enormous financial difficulties that are complicated even further by a reduced income. This has placed substantial pressure on the government unemployment benefit programs and social service agencies. Many people are finding their lives changed by these trends at a dizzying rate.

The Significance of Performance Evaluations

When performance evaluations first came into use they were badly needed. They filled a void when employees had no official way of knowing how they were doing on the job. Performance evaluations benefited employees by giving them the opportunity to meet with their employer to discuss their status, their contributions, any shortcomings, and how they could improve.

Unfortunately, it is also possible for employers to use this device to rid the payroll of employees who have a long record of satisfactory to excellent service. They purposely lower the ratings and use words like *unsatisfactory* whether or not there has been an actual change in the level of performance.

If you see this happening, be alert; it could be an indicator of things to come. According to the *AARP Bulletin*, a publication of the American Association of Retired Persons, "The words matter. Not only do you kiss good-bye that raise and promotion, you can't even keep your job."

Some employees claim that appraisals are misused against older workers. Some employers have been taken to court and complaints have been filed with the Equal Employment Opportunity Commission. Performance evaluations are designed to be objective and impartial. In most cases, they help the employee.

The important thing to remember is that if you see a sudden change in your review, watch out. There are many subtle ways of anticipating layoffs and early retirements. Be sensitive to any signals you may get. Many people have been caught completely by surprise when they were laid off, simply because they did not recognize the early signals.

Retirement

Changes in the work force due to retirements, both voluntary and involuntary, are growing with each year that passes. One of the most discriminating policies in some organizations is mandatory retirement at the age of 65. This arbitrary age was set in Germany when the social security system was first established under Bismarck. While many people look forward to retiring at 65 or earlier, it causes great hardships for others.

Financial and emotional stress, along with a lack of purpose, frequently lead to shortened lives. Commerce and industry have deprived themselves of a great amount of talent by terminating the careers of potentially highly productive people. Mandatory retirement is not always legal; however, employers still find ways to get around the law.

When approaching retirement it is wise to do some planning. You probably will want to work at *something* when you retire; so develop and test hobbies and interests before retiring to make sure they are feasible and practical to pursue. Observe other retirees to avoid mistakes they may have made, and recognize that a retirement plan that is ideal for one person is not necessarily good for another. Retirement options must be custom designed to the individual's personality, interests, physical well-being, marital status, and financial condition. Properly planned retirement can be a wonderful change of pace. It can be a period of relaxation, enjoyment, and fulfillment; or, it can be a disaster filled with frustration, insecurity, financial problems, and reduced longevity. The difference lies in how you approach it.

Fortunately, the 1990s should provide more types of job and career choices than in the recent past. Employers are becoming more flexible about alternatives to the typical nine to five work day. It also may become more cost efficient for employers to keep employees on their payrolls rather than pay their retirement and other benefits. For economic reasons, second careers will become popular. Already, for example, retirees are filling part-time jobs as clerks and food service workers. In the future, employees will retire to accept jobs with less pressure and fewer time requirements. They can combine their leisure time interests with work that provides them with additional finances, personal contacts and reduced pressures.

Retirees who have lump sum settlements at retirement may use their payments to travel or start their own business. They may do what they wanted to do earlier in life but could not because of work constraints. A whole new field of entrepreneurs will develop through these retirement benefits.

Being retired by a large corporation can be especially painful because corporate culture has encouraged the idea of loyalty— the feeling of family, the security, the trappings, the idea of going to the office. "Some people shift to a self-employed or entrepreneurial status because they truly enjoy independence," says Phyllis Macklin, a partner of Minsuk, Macklin, Stein, and Associates of Princeton Junction, who specializes in **outplacement**. "But if a still-angry dismissed employee says he wants to be on his own because he says he never wants to work for a company again," she tries to discourage him. "We have to get him to look for something to go to rather than escape from."

Plan for Your Retirement

A decade ago, the target age for retirement was 65. Most corporations and employers geared themselves for retirement at that age. This is not so today. Many choose to retire or are forced to retire before the age of 65, while others have their eyes set on working as long as they feel good. Work, enjoyable work, has become a mainstay of their existence, and they feel working is a far better option than leisure time.

Retirement brings many changes. Changes in hours, income, contacts, status, leisure time, priorities, **regimentation**, environment, etc. Not everyone can cope with all these changes. This increases the importance of thinking through all the aspects of retirement. Planning for retirement should be done years in advance of your retirement date to minimize the impact of the changes that will take place. Chapter Four will help you identify your interests and the best sources of opportunities for you. Talk with those who have already retired to help you understand the advantages and disadvantages of retirement. What is right for some people may be wrong for others. Only you can truly identify what is good for you—then act accordingly.

Don't **procrastinate**. Think and plan early so that when the time comes, you will be in control. As you make your plans, keep these guidelines in mind:

1. Risk taking is **inevitable**. Don't be afraid to let go of the past and look to the future.

2. Be thorough in your self-assessment. You will have to base your decision upon this information.

3. If you decide to change employers, carry out your job search with total commitment.

4. Discuss the options with your spouse to make sure the plans are compatible with him or her.

5. Assume that the days ahead can be the best years of your life if you work things out properly.

Self-Directed Mid-Career Change

If you decide to make a change, or if you are forced to make a change, be **aggressive** in seeking another opportunity. A self-directed career change involves taking responsibility for your own decisions and actions, and not expecting others to direct your career. This does not mean that you cannot seek the help of others in determining your career path—it means simply accepting the responsibility for your career. Also, remember to give yourself plenty of lead time. It usually takes six months or longer to make a good mid-career change.

Sometimes people who know they need a job change simply let others direct their career. They leave all the decisions to their boss, their relatives, their peers, their company, or their government. Then they blame others if they are not happy with the results.

Procrastination is another means of avoiding the responsibility of self-direction. It is easy to procrastinate when making a job change. There always seems to be some other priority that gets in the way of taking immediate action. In reality, procrastination is often based on a fear of risk taking, inconvenience, or an unwillingness to make a difficult decision. Overcome these **obstacles** and you are well on your way toward making a change. Actually, getting fired is often a blessing in disguise; it overcomes all the obstacles mentioned above and forces you to get on with your career.

For most people, making a job change need not be the problem they envision. They may find it temporarily inconvenient, but in the long run, it is not as traumatic as they imagined. Most people are glad they made the decision.

Personality plays an important role in a self-directed career. Confidence, economics, and willingness to change are the biggest factors in directing your career. **Rationalization**, procrastination, and failure to take risks are the biggest pitfalls.

The secret lies in *getting on with it* once you decide a change is necessary. The decision is yours and yours alone. Don't clutter your decision to act with **extraneous** factors. First, decide if you are going to make the change. Once you make that decision, and if the answer is yes, plan to move forward with a total commitment to making the change, regardless of the effort required. Procrastination will get you nowhere. Beware of it and get on with your change. That is the self-directed approach.

What Does Success Mean to You?

Success is a highly individualized matter. Wealth, fame and power have been suggested, in various combinations, as possible definitions of success. But even these cannot be the standard for everyone. For most people, success at work is closely related to success in life. However, some see personal success exclusively in terms of their work. This can be a mistake.

What, then, makes for a successful career? The ingredients differ for everyone. In addition to wealth, fame, and power, they might also include: decision making, enthusiasm for the work, specific skills, independence, health considerations, family implications, geo- graphical location, and personal satis- faction. Others say they are looking for a new sense of dignity and meaning in their work.

Successful people have certain character- istics. One of those characteristics is the desire to get ahead. Choosing a field of work that you enjoy has built-in **motivational** factors that enhance the potential for success. Successful people believe strongly in their ability to get things done. Many people fail to achieve their goals because they do not believe enough in themselves or their objective.

Successful people know a lot about their work; they know their part of the business better than others. They usually are ahead of their competition in determining the markets for their products and services. They work hard and enjoy it. Sometimes this is at the expense of family and good health. There is much to be said for those who work hard. However, when it affects the family or an individual's health, the word *success* becomes tarnished and that person may not be successful at all. It depends upon what is important to you.

Successful people are usually risk takers. They take calculated risks based on a combination of intuition, instinct, experience, knowledge, creativity, and plain courage.

People who are successful often are influenced by someone else. That person might be a parent, a teacher, a friend, a fellow worker, or a mentor. Influential people help others by setting a good example, offering advice, or simply offering encouragement at an appropriate time. Cultivate such contacts and maintain them if possible. Do not, however, rely on another person as your sole key to the future. This person may help you, but you are the one responsible for your destiny. Look to yourself for the pathway to success.

In order to define success, you must know yourself. This is not easy, but it is the secret to finding the right career for you. You need to be aware of your likes, dislikes, values, abilities, and all those other factors that are unique to your character. You are well on your way to a successful career if you know yourself. Employers dangle money, prestige, promotions, titles, awards, and many other **incentives** before employees.

If the job you select has the incentives you want, go after it. If the incentives your potential employer offers represent false goals, recognize them as such, and go on from there. In the long run, you will be more successful and happy. This principle is so simple, but it is amazing how many people ignore it until it is too late in their careers to do anything about it.

As you proceed down your career path, remember that the choices you make are like playing a game of chess. Each move has an impact on all future moves. You cannot avoid the consequences of your decisions—they have far more impact on your future happiness than most can imagine. Make good decisions and good results will follow.

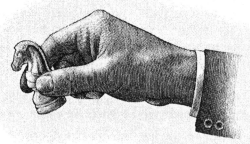

Questions for Review

1. Name 15 factors you should consider before making a job change.

2. What are your options to consider before making the decision to change employers.

3. What are the advantages of making a career change within your organization?

4. Will there be an increase in the number of workers, between the ages of 35 and 54, by the year 2000? If so, by how much?

5. What are some of the things you should be thinking about as you approach retirement?

6. What is a self-directed mid-career change?

7. What is the secret of finding the right career for you?

Chapter Four:

Self-Assessment

Thales was asked what was most difficult to man;
he answered: "To know oneself."

Diogenes

Know Yourself

Anyone facing career change will be more likely to succeed if his or her decisions are based upon accurate self-assessment and a continuing desire to grow professionally. Most of us have talents and abilities that must be cultivated for us to reach our full potential. You must believe these talents exist. Self-assessment helps you understand your abilities. It helps you recognize your strengths and weaknesses; it helps you discover talents that you did not know you had; and it can open up new horizons and realign your career objectives. Only when you carefully study your talents and achievements can you use them to reach your potential.

Unfortunately, many people never take the time to assess their true capabilities or analyze what is most important or satisfying to them. As a result, they may spend years working at jobs for which they are not well suited, or that they do not enjoy.

Too many people fail to plan for the future. Instead, they rely solely on chance to present them with job opportunities. By doing this, they can be forced to compromise more than they should. Very often people accept a job purely for financial reasons. Although the new position appears to be a good opportunity, after working in the job for a short time they learn it is not what they hoped it would be. Soon they may be looking to change again. This is a common pattern, and is related to the tendency to base decisions upon short-term, reactive considerations. Instead of positive career growth, it usually results only in repeated job changing.

It is unrealistic to expect that all of the jobs in your career path will be everything you hope for. However, deliberate and conscientious **self-direction** based upon **objective self-assessment** generally leads to greater fulfillment in most jobs. Self-direction requires careful analysis and planning regarding your career path and what is important to you professionally. This does not mean you will be able to do everything you want or earn as much as you desire in every position. Nevertheless, taking the time to think about what is important to you, what your skills are, what types of positions match these factors, and using this information to make career decisions increases your chances of having a fulfilling career.

Self-direction is related to self-discipline. Most people simply react to the flow of daily events. They do this in response to events in their careers as well as in response to personal difficulties and challenges. Reaction is an important part of maturity. The ability to react in a resourceful manner helps us cope with life. However, a behavioral pattern of merely reacting to events on a day to day basis provides little chance for long-term professional or personal growth.

The tendency simply to react to life instead of facing major issues or anticipating and preparing for them is often due to a lack of self-discipline or control. Initially, spontaneous reaction may appear to be less painful than preparation, and may explain why so many people seem to choose that method of dealing with challenges. In *The Road Less Traveled* (New York: Simon and Schuster, 1978), M. Scott Peck, M.D., discusses the **dilemma** all adults face in confronting and solving life's challenges. He suggests that solving difficult challenges (personal and career related) can be painful; and as a result, many try to avoid such confrontation.

> *"The issue is important, because many people simply do not take the time necessary to solve many of life's intellectual, social, or spiritual problems . . . It is the hope that problems will go away of their own accord."*

Facing challenges requires taking time to gather facts, and then basing decisions upon such facts. When facing the challenge of a career change, self-assessment is essential to gathering facts about your capabilities as well as any shortcomings you may need to overcome.

Self-direction requires self-discipline, conscientious **intro- spection**, and a desire for growth. A self-directed person is someone who assumes complete responsibility for his or her motivation and ultimate success or setbacks. This does not mean that you should not seek assistance from others, or look for spiritual or religious guidance. However, it is your deliberate and purposeful action based upon objective self- assessment that will ultimately determine your success in life. Many people never realize this and simply depend upon the action of others. Then, when things do not work out the way they hoped, they blame other people or circumstances for their troubles.

Fear often accompanies a lack of self-direction in two different forms. The first type of fear is *insecurity*. Some people are so intimidated by change, potential loss of income, or upsetting their spouse, they are paralyzed into inaction even when they hold a job which makes them miserable. The second type of fear is *avoidance*. Many people focus more upon what they don't want in life, than what they do want. They become more oriented toward avoiding new challenges than assuming them.

As a result, fear is what rules people without self-direction. After allowing fear to seriously restrict their career, financial, and personal options, they choose from what is left—which usually isn't too much.

Career-Related Self-Assessment Techniques

If you understand yourself and base your work behavior and career planning upon such knowledge, you are more likely to succeed. Self-assessment is a critical part of adjusting to your current work setting. Self-assessment never really ends. It is an attitude in which you constantly strive to understand yourself better, and think carefully about the opportunities that are available to you. Self-assessment is part of a growing and maturing process that should occur throughout the entire span of your career.

There are many different types and methods of self-assessment. The kind you use will depend on the information you desire and the situation you want to evaluate. The context we will focus upon yields information required for career change decisions.

Self-assessment includes three different dimensions: (1) **qualifications** (marketable skills), (2) **interests** (values and goals), and (3) **interpersonal style** (interactive ability). Such factors can help you understand your potential, what you would like to do with it, and the likelihood of enlisting others to help you attain it. See Figure 4-1.

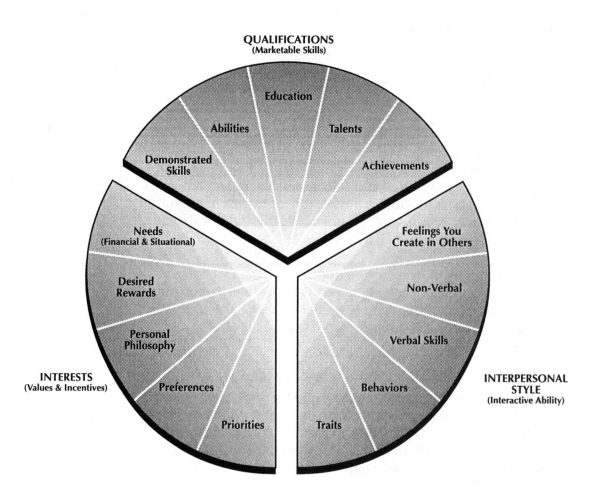

Figure 4-1

Your qualifications are your marketable skills and any other traits you possess that prepare you to do a job. **Marketable skills** are your talents. These are the demonstrable tasks, learned skills, and abilities you have handled in previous jobs or in other situations. They are the things you are very capable of doing. They may also include activities you have potential for performing although you may not have been paid for them in a job. Marketable skills also include specific educational, technical, or achievement credentials. It may be important to have other people serve as references for you regarding those skills if you are interviewing for a new position.

Potential marketable skills are abilities you possess which are transferrable to another job. For example, if you have a great deal of experience at selling computer software programs, and this experience required preparation of written materials and follow-up presentations, it is reasonable to assume you may also be qualified to become a trainer for a software firm—even though you have never held such a position. This is an example of a transferrable skill. Although you have not been paid for doing it, you have potential for performing it.

It is important to assess your interests carefully as well. Your interests are influenced by your values and goals. They determine your likes and dislikes in the work setting. Again, this is an ongoing assessment. Though your values will probably remain consistent over a long period of time, there will be different, specific rewards or incentives that are important to you at different times. It is important for you to have an accurate perception of your interests, including values and incentives, at all times. If you do not, you may lose sight of what is most important to you along the way.

Interpersonal style is the third dimension of assessment. It refers to the behaviors and characteristics that are unique to you and that reflect your personality. Interpersonal style refers to those traits and characteristics that shape the way other people view you. When we describe someone, we normally do not refer to specific behavioral traits of the individual. We are more likely to refer to how we feel about them. Is he a nice person? Is he aggressive? Is he strong willed? It is our behaviors and traits which create these impressions and feelings in others.

Assessment of your interpersonal style is necessary in at least two primary areas regarding your career path. First, it helps to have a good understanding of your interactive ability as you face interviews regarding career opportunities. If you understand the impact of your interpersonal style, it gives you a tremendous advantage in terms of capitalizing on your strengths and overcoming your weaknesses. This is particularly helpful in interviews. Second, in most jobs or work situations, your interactive ability is critical to your success in dealing with other people; therefore, it has a direct impact upon your career success. Here is an actual case study of a young man who discovered a deficiency in his ability to interact with others. This is not the man's real name.

Case Study—Tom Fisher

After thirty years of career success in financial management, Tom Fisher felt secure in his position as the Business Planning Manager for Europe and Latin America at one of the Big Three automotive firms. His earnings history, the status of his position, and his reputation all seemed to indicate that he had achieved a winning formula in his career path.

However, below the surface, problems were developing that would soon affect Tom and his staff. His company, like so many automotive industry firms, had been struggling with difficult business challenges in the past few years. Unfavorable business conditions had already caused a large number of professional managers to lose their jobs.

However, what placed Tom in jeopardy of losing his position was not so much the fact that his company was reducing its number of executives, as much as the fact that his personality was working against him. Over the years, Tom had fought his way to the top with long hours, shrewd business decisions and a less than tactful manner. In fact, he had used abrasive and hostile tactics in many confrontations which he called "battles with the bureaucracy." As long as the firm was flourishing, political considerations were not quite so critical, and his supervisors were willing to overlook his behavior.

With tougher business conditions, his company had to reduce the number of professionals in his earnings bracket, and because of his attitude, Tom was soon targeted for early retirement. He was shocked when his boss told him he was being replaced. When he asked why, he was told bluntly that he simply had **alienated** too many people above and below him to continue in his present capacity.

He was offered an option of early retirement or a temporary demotion. When he asked what was meant by *temporary*, he was told that he would be given a trial period in a lower paying position, but unless his interactive style improved, he would lose his job completely. Because he had always been a fighter, Tom was determined to hang on and do what was necessary to work his way back up.

After much introspection, and with the support of his new boss, the Vice President of Truck Operations, he decided to seek assistance in strengthening his interactive skills. He came to this decision on his own when he realized that an important facet of his executive skills had never developed as it should.

Tom began to work with a management consultant his firm had retained to assist other managers and executives in strengthening their executive skills. After 12 months of structured self-assessment and assistance from the consultant, Tom began to overcome some of the critical interpersonal shortcomings that had been working against him.

Tom never left his employer and has been promoted twice since his demotion. This true case illustrates the fact that no professional, no matter how late in their career, is beyond the potential for significant growth. However, he or she must have the desire to improve, remain open to self-assessment, and take a fresh look at himself or herself. More importantly, career change does not necessarily require leaving a current employer. Sometimes a simple change within the individual is all that is necessary for career satisfaction.

Assessing Your Marketable Skills

In assessing your marketable skills, begin by listing the types of skills you possess in the order in which you acquired them. You can start with your earliest experience right out of school and bring it up to present. This is not a resume. It is simply a listing of the jobs including the specific tasks and duties you have handled.

For example, if your first position was working as a clerk in a bank, you should write down the general heading of clerk. Then you would list all of the specific tasks and duties in that position. Be sure to include them all—whether it was reconciling statements, making record entries, posting entries on balance sheets, or whatever. Don't worry about how much time you spent working in the position. Be more concerned with the tasks and activities in which you know you were competent. List each job you have held up to the present day.

Once you have completed this list, you will need to go back
and highlight those skills and activities in which you were the
most competent, as well as those which you consider to be
transferrable skills. Next, identify the medium and low competence categories. This type of rating scheme will help you
make decisions on new career options and identify your
strengths to be brought up in interviews. Be fair to yourself,
but do not list abilities that your really do not have. If you
stretch the range of your abilities too far, you will probably
find yourself travelling down a career path for which you are
not well suited.

Once you have identified your specific marketable skills,
including those tasks and activities you have had much experience with, as well as those you consider to be transferrable
skills, you will be prepared to move on to listing education or
achievement credentials. Include all of the formal degrees or
certifications you received for educational programs. Also
include any specific achievements for which you received
formal recognition. For example, if you were awarded the top
sales honor in an organization for a
particular month or sales period,
include that as well.

One technique that
might help you assess
your marketable skills
is to talk with friends,
peers and associates
who know you well.
Often, people who
have worked with you
can provide accurate
observations regard-
ing your capabilities
that you may not see.
They may help you

enhance your potential qualifications, or they may provide
more objective perspective in respect to skills you thought
you had. In addition to gaining insight from others, you may
decide you would like to take some standardized tests that
are designed to assess skills, aptitudes, or abilities. There are
various types of **aptitude tests** and **skills assessment inventories** on the market. If you use them, the assistance of a
trained counselor is recommended. There are sources listed
in Appendix F to help you get started.

Listing marketable skills can help you develop an inventory of
what you have to offer potential employers. It can also provide
you with a more objective view in regarding the diversity and
depth of your background. Also, by thinking carefully about
what you have done so far, and by gaining the perspective of
others, you are more likely to develop ideas for related or new
pursuits. Here is an example of one young woman's list of
marketable skills. This is an actual case study, but we have
changed the woman's name.

Marketable Skills List for Sue Grant

After earning her Bachelor of Arts degree in Education from a
large midwestern university, Sue Grant began teaching high
school English. She taught for only two years before taking a
position as a communications specialist at a State Department
of Commerce. She held various positions with the Department
of Commerce over a ten-year period, including production chief
of monthly newsletters, public relations director, several training positions, and a supervisory position in the personnel
department.

As she reviewed all of the duties required of her previous
positions, including specific tasks, activities, and what she
considered transferable skills, she developed the following
list. Notice that she breaks the list down according to high,
medium and low competence.

HIGH COMPETENCE SKILLS

Writing copy for news releases, advertisements, or speeches.
Stand-up training (professional subjects).
Handling media relations
Development of public relations strategy and policy
On-camera presentations
Public speaking (large, live audiences)
Chairing professional committees

MEDIUM COMPETENCE SKILLS

Interpersonal supervision of professional employees
Coordinating administrative functions
Working with young adults (under age 18)
Research skills
Planning and coordinating conventions of professional meetings
Coordinating media events
Directing membership drives

LOW COMPETENCE SKILLS

Preparing analytical reports
Data analysis
Preparing or working with budgets
Writing reports on quantitative subjects
Monitoring resource allocations

Figure 4-2: Marketable Skills List

It is important to note that she includes medium and low competence skills assessment. This helps her gain a sense of those areas in which she may be cautious when considering new positions—even though she had experience in these areas. Medium and low competence skills may also point out areas that she may want to work on in the future.

Assessment of Values

Values assessment is one of the most difficult tasks you will face. The reason it is hard to identify priority values for ourselves is because they are so **subjective**. By values, we mean the degree of importance a person places on events, materials, philosophies, right or wrong, or any specific entity. Your values have tremendous impact upon your incentives and interests.

Values assessment is important because unless you systematically review what is important to you, it is very likely that emotions, current situations, or daily circumstances may tend to mask your awareness of your basic values. As a result, your conscious view of what is important may vary widely from day to day or week to week and cause you to lose sight of what is most critical to you in the long run.

By systematically reviewing your values, writing them down and using them to help you develop priorities, you are more likely to reach important long-term goals and objectives. This will force you to think carefully about your interests and the decisions you make. Unless you keep your goals in mind, it is easy to stray from them.

For example, a higher salary or a different geographical location may seem most important to you, but if the job doesn't satisfy your real needs in terms of values, you will not be happy with it. Think of the big picture before making any career changes. Consider the fact that earning a little more money in another job may have little value if it means giving up what you have. If you look at the complete situation, and recognize your values, you are more likely to have a more realistic perspective on which to base your decisions.

Interpersonal Assessment

Assessment of your interpersonal skills can be a revealing and interesting experience. By gaining a realistic perspective of your interpersonal skills, you are provided with a decided advantage in terms of how you relate to others. It is difficult for us to see ourselves the way others see us. We often have many subjective perceptions about the impression we convey to other people which are not totally accurate. Sometimes, our view of our own interpersonal skills is so biased that we may not have a realistic conception of how we are viewed by others. It is very difficult to gain this perspective by yourself.

There are a number of different methods available today that can help you gain a realistic perspective of your interpersonal skills. Licensed career counselors are an excellent source for gaining access to such tools. See Appendix F. Regardless of whether you use a formal approach or not, it is important to gain some perspective on your interpersonal skills from other people in a systematic way.

While we do not recommend that you walk up to your best friend or a co-worker and say, "How do I make you feel?" or "How do you feel about me?" this is actually what you are trying to learn. The way other people feel about you and the feelings you convey to them are critical to your career success. Your interpersonal skills will have a great impact upon your ability to interview for jobs or talk with other people about career opportunities for yourself. In addition, your interpersonal skills are going to be a significant advantage or disadvantage to you in terms of your professional experience.

Interpersonal skills can, in part, be described by specific behaviors you demonstrate. For example, do you speak quickly or slowly? This is an activity that is observable by other people, and it often affects how others feel about you. Speaking patterns, facial expressions, posture, the amount of aggressiveness or assertiveness you demonstrate, and any other observable activities that you demonstrate create your unique behavioral pattern. They determine how other people feel about you.

People interact and express themselves continuously in a number of ways, only one of them being speech. There is a constant flow of visual, **tactile**, and auditory information transmitted and interpreted (consciously and unconsciously) through interaction. Dr. Albert Mehrabian, a former faculty member and researcher at the University of California, has identified three dimensions of face-to-face communication including verbal, vocal, and facial. According to his research, the impact of each can be assigned as follows: 7% of our interpersonal impact is verbal (what we say); 38% is vocal (how we say it, including tone of voice); 55% facial (how we look and act). The majority of communication (a total of 93% according to Dr. Mehrabian), is non-verbal.

Various levels of non-verbal skills are required for different professional activities. Some occupations require good non-verbal skills. For example, a person who works as a supervisory skills trainer or group facilitator would normally require much stronger non-verbal skills than a bookkeeper. Regardless of your chosen career direction or occupation, non-verbal skills will play an important role, even if it is only during job interviews.

Interpersonal skills also relate to the way you react to others. For example, if you tell somebody you are interested in what they have to say, maintain eye contact, and nod your head, but do not follow through with a reply, you are sending conflicting messages. Your observable behaviors say you are listening. However, if you do not act or respond in appropriately, you may convince them that you are not a good listener or that you may not be truthful.

In order to gain a valid assessment of your interpersonal skills, you can gain objective information from at least three sources. First, carefully observe the ways in which other people respond to you. Do they seem to be interested in what you communicate? Do their behaviors indicate their interest or at least their attention? Look for a pattern. Second, tactfully seek information from others you know well and respect. You do not have to accept what each says, but listen carefully, consider their perspective, and look to see if it is consistent with what others tell you. A third source is through formal assessment instruments such as tests, inventories, and questionnaires which may be administered by trained counselors.

Regardless of what sources you use, the important thing is to become more aware of how you affect others and to understand your strengths and weaknesses in interpersonal settings. This knowledge will provide you with a significant advantage in achieving career success.

Questions to Ask Yourself
When Considering a Mid-Career Change

The following questions can be instrumental in self-assessment for a mid-career change. It is important that you respond to these in an objective and honest way. If you do, the insight regarding your likes, dislikes, skills, and values will better prepare you for making a career change.

1. What are your specific reasons for wanting to make a career change?

2. Do you think you are missing something in your present job? What?

3. Do you like the organization for which you work?

4. Do you like your supervisor?

5. Have you had conflicts with others in the workplace? If so, is this why you want a change?

6. Are you overworked in your current job?

7. Can you correct problems in your workplace by a discussing them with your supervisor or employer?

8. Do you feel you have plateaued in your current job?

9. What are your present promotional opportunities?

10. What are the disadvantages of your current job?

11. Do you have the opportunity for independent thought and action in your current job?

12. Do you get enough physical activity in your job?

13. Do you have enough diversity in your work?

14. Do you enjoy the environment in which you work?

15. Do you have a sense of accomplishment in your current job?

16. Have you had any failures at work? If so, what were they?

17. What is your current job title and what job title do you want?

18. Is your current job stressful? If so, what makes it stressful?

19. Have you experienced any health problems from your work?

20. Have you exhausted all the potential career opportunities with your current employer?

21. Do you have job security at present?

22. How important is job security to you?

23. Are you being replaced by technological advances?

24. Are you being "let go" by the employer? If so, for what reason?

25. Has your present job become near obsolete?

26. Are you discouraged by the future opportunities of your current job?

27. Were you ever fired? If so, what were the reasons?

28. Did you quit your job? If so, what were your reasons?

29. Do you enjoy your occupation?

30. Are you proud of your occupation?

31. Do you want more or less responsibility?

32. Do you want to change jobs because you want to change careers?

33. If you are dissatisfied with your current occupation, what don't you like about it?

34. Do you wish you had chosen a different career? If so, what?

35. Is prestige on the job important to you?

36. If you could choose to do anything in the world with your time, what would you do?

37. Do you prefer to work for a large company or a small company?

38.   Do you think you have maximized the use of your talents?

39.   If you are currently dissatisfied with your life or career, with what are you dissatisfied?

40.   Do you have another career opportunity available to you? If so, considering the questions on this list, how does it compare to your current position?

41.   Are you prepared to make a dramatic change in careers (physically and mentally)?

42.   Will a career change have an effect on your social life?

43.   Will a change in career change your personal priorities?

44.   What are the things that are most important to you in life?

45.   Are you satisfied with your life outside of your work?

46.   Do you spend enough time with your family?

47.   Do you have enough time for leisure activities?

48.   How do you describe your general level of happiness?

49.   What are looking for in life?

50.   Have you taken enough time to reflect on where you are, where you have been, and where you want to go?

51.   Does your spouse want you to make a change?

52.   Does your marital status or situation have anything to do with your wanting to change careers?

53.   Will your change in jobs impact your spouse's career?

54.   Would you consider moving to another part of the country?

55.   If you change jobs, how will it affect your family (moving, schools, etc.)?

56.   Are you satisfied with the geographical area where you work? If not, what area would you prefer?

57.   What is the minimum salary you need if the ideal job is available?

58.   Are you prepared to make a dramatic change in careers from an economic standpoint?

59.   If early retirement (with benefits) is available, do you want to work full-time or part-time?

60.   Do you currently have a good retirement program?

61.   Are you at a point in your life where you want to "take it easy?"

62.   At what age do you want to stop working full-time? Part-time?

63.   Are you planning on early retirement? If so, what are your plans during early retirement?

64.   If you plan early retirement, will your retirement income be sufficient for your needs?

65.   Have you spoken to early retirees to get their advice?

66.   Have you spoken to late retirees to get their advice?

67.   Would you describe yourself as a workaholic?

68.   Do you prefer to work alone or with other people?

69.   Do you like to do things for others?

70.   Do you enjoy risk-taking?

71.   Does your personality affect your job? If so, what do you consider to be the good and bad points?

72.   Do you avoid situations that are unpredictable?

73.   Generally, are you a positive person?

74.   Do you adjust to change readily?

75.   What do you consider to be your shortcomings?

76. Have you kept up with the technological changes in your field of work?

77. Do you need additional training or education to enter the field you would like to enter?

78. What are your best assets?

79. What are your most marketable skills?

80. Do you feel you have enough formal education for your career expectations?

81. Do you want to be self-employed? If so, what has stopped you from starting your own business in the past?

82. Is this an appropriate time to try to become self-employed?

83. If you want to become self-employed, have you spoken with others who have started a similar business?

84. Are you aware of the time and effort usually required to make a career change? Are you prepared to commit to that amount of time and effort?

85. Do you understand that the person responsible for your career change is you, and you alone?

86. What is your plan for making a mid-career change?

87. Do you believe your answers to these questions have been accurate and objective?

What Would You Like to Do?

People seeking a mid-career change often have a difficult time pinpointing exactly what type of job they would like. If you encounter this problem, try listing the types of things you like to do. Your list may suggest the type of work you should pursue. This premise will provide you with a direction in which to start. If you are doing what you like to do, chances are you will be successful at it. If you are doing something that you don't enjoy, chances are you will not be happy; and if you are unhappy, you cannot be truly successful.

Remember—the American dream of fame, fortune, and power is not necessarily the definition of success for everyone. Define success on your own terms, by your own value system. Do not accept a definition that society, your employer, your friends, or your relatives have given you.

Assessment Activities

1. Valid self-assessment will include the help of other
    people and sources to gain a realistic perspective on
    your marketability, values, and interpersonal skills.
    List the people and sources who may be helpful to you
    in this manner and plan to contact them.

2. Assess your marketable skills by identifying the areas
    and skills with which you have experience, the areas
    for which you have potential (transferrable skills), and
    your educational or achievement credentials. Prepare
    a list and rate your competence in each area.

3. Values assessment requires a systematic review of the
    priorities you give events, materials, philosophies, or
    other individual considerations. Examine and develop
    a written list of your values in order of priority.

4. Remember, interpersonal assessment is best achieved
    through introspection, from the perspective of others,
    and through the assistance of licensed counselors.
    You may choose from any of these options—or apply all
    three—to gain valuable perspective upon this important
    facet of your personality.

Questions for Review

1. Describe the three dimensions of self-assessment.

2. Why is values assessment important in considering a career change?

3. Describe self-direction and its role in developing a positive career path.

4. What techniques might you use to assess your marketable skills?

5. Why is understanding your interpersonal style important when thinking of making a career change?

Chapter Five:

Exploring the Market

If men could regard the events of their lives with more
open minds they would frequently discover that they
did not really desire the things they failed to obtain.
                                    Andre Maurois
                                    The Art of Living

Understanding the Job Market

When planning to change careers, people frequently use one of two sources. First, they look at advertisements in the classified ads of a local newspaper. Second, they check to see if they know somebody who is aware of a job for which they can apply. These methods produce results for a number of people. However, focusing only upon them can be very restricting in the search for new opportunities. Before making a change in your career, you should explore the market carefully to find out what opportunities are available.

Identifying Opportunities

Your **job market** consists of the jobs that are interesting to you, the jobs for which you are qualified, and the jobs that meet your goals in terms of situation, opportunity, and financial considerations. There is no *general market*. You may hear that the market is good or bad, but it depends upon what you do and what is in demand. There is almost always a good employment market for those who excel in their field. Although there may be peaks and slumps at different times within a given field, regardless of the market, the most critical things for you to understand are which of your skills are in demand and how to market them.

Your basic objective in exploring the market is to find out what kinds of opportunities exist and where they are likely to be found. If you take the time to do the job properly, you will:

1. Determine a focus for your effort once you begin the job hunt. You will learn where the most likely sources of opportunity are likely to be and how you can position yourself to gain access. This will be defined in terms of industries, geographic regions, types of positions, etc. Sometimes, the best opportunities are with smaller companies; these employers usually are more flexible and receptive to innovative ideas.

2. Identify the most likely companies or organizations to have a need and interest in people with your qualifications. Develop a detailed list of contacts and use it when you look for specific openings.

3. Gather information on the organizations with which you interview. You want to be as informed as possible when you interview. Do not limit your research to company literature available in the reception area. Do your homework thoroughly prior to the interview.

4. Develop job search skills. No one book or manual can meet all the informational needs of everyone who reads it and still maintain its focus. Pursue specific topics of interest through reference books, knowledgeable individuals, and classes to make sure you are prepared.

5. Diagnose potential openings before they are formally established. By observing trends and business events in existing and new businesses and industries, you may gain a sense of who is likely to need additional people in the near future. Watch for news of awards on new contracts, acquisitions, mergers, relocations, and expansions. These often reveal potential openings.

Beginning Your Research

How does a person identify the best sources of information?
A public library is a good place to start. Obviously, you will
not be able, nor want, to explore all the options that are
available. The sources you use will
depend on your interests.
A good source will help
you gain a clear per-
spective on the career
paths you intend to
research. The library
holds three important
sources of information;
trade publications,
periodical indexes,
and various **reference
directories**. Use
them to develop lists
of organizations you
intend to contact.
Look, not only for
names and addresses of key
contacts within the organization, but for telephone numbers
as well. In addition, look for key contacts in industries that
interest you even if they do not work for organizations you
would consider. They may be excellent sources of advice.

Trade Publications

All industries and professions have publications targeted at
the people who are employed in them. Trade publications
include newspapers, magazines, journals, and newsletters.
These publications are an excellent source of information on
employment trends and opportunities, as well as industry
developments, issues, key contacts, recruiters, and more.
The newspapers, magazines, and journals can be found by
consulting *Business Publication Rates & Data* (Standard Rate

& Data Service) or the *Standard Periodical Directory* (Oxbridge Publishing Co.). Try to become familiar with at least three publications for each industry or profession you are researching. Consult them at least once a month during the entire course of your career change.

Periodical Indexes

Industry trends can help you decide where the best opportunities may lie for you. While researching such information may not be absolutely necessary, you may find it helpful. An excellent source of industry trends is articles written on developments, issues, and forecasts within industries, companies and professions. You can access this information by consulting periodical indexes in the library.

Consider using at least three periodical indexes in your search. These may include:

- *Predicasts F&S Index, United States* (Predicasts, Inc.). This source provides abstracts and indexes of over 1000 trade journals, business and financial publications, government reports, newspapers and other sources.

- *Business Periodicals Index* (H. W. Wilson Co.). Here you will gain access to articles from *Fortune*, *Business Week*, *Forbes*, and others on company performance, career opportunities, employment trends and more.

- Newspaper Indexes. Indexes by newspapers such as the *New York Times*, *Chicago Tribune*, and the *Wall Street Journal*. Incidentally, the *Wall Street Journal* publishes its own compilation of career information including hundreds of job openings in the *National Business Employment Weekly*. This is an excellent source for almost anyone seeking a career change.

Reference Directories

Reference directories provide lists of subjects and tell you how to obtain information on these subjects. They will help you develop networks of people, companies, and organizations to contact. They can also provide basic inside information on companies and organizations such as names of executives, statistics on financials, etc.

There are at least three basic reference directories with which you should become familiar. These include:

- The *Encyclopedia of Associations* (Gale Research Company)

- The *Encyclopedia of Business Information Sources* (Gale Research Company)

- *Directories in Print* (Gale Research Company)

By consulting most business libraries, you can find a copy of the *Encyclopedia of Associations*. This publication provides information on thousands of professional associations and lists addresses and telephone numbers. Associations are an excellent starting point from which to gain perspective on the demand for your skill areas. Remember, demand is described not only in terms of the number of required people in specific skill areas over a period of time, but also geographic concentration, expected incomes, etc. Be sure to consider these factors carefully as you do your research.

The *Encyclopedia of Business Information Sources* is a general directory which lists newsletters, magazines, handbooks and related sources on over 1,000 business topics. It is not as complete as some other directories, but provides quick access to subjects. It is often a good place to start general research efforts.

Directories in Print is a list of almost 8,000 directories according to industry and general business. This directory will help you identify specific sources for research in those industries you want to learn more about. Like the *Encyclopedia of Business Information Sources*, use it early in your research to establish the direction of your search.

Further Research

As you begin to narrow the focus of your research, you should identify the industries, professions, companies, and organizations that most represent the kinds of opportunities that interest you. Once you establish your specific interests, continued research will give you the information you need to set employment goals (i.e., who to contact, the types of positions you seek, earnings levels, etc.).

It may be important to consult both industry-specific and corporate directories, depending upon your focus. Industry-specific directories are guides or manuals that list companies or organizations within an industry. The listings are in alphabetical order. You can use these directories to develop a list of those companies that fall into your desired employment area. Corporate directories will then assist you in learning more about those companies you may be interested in contacting.

Examples of corporate directories include *Moody's Industrial Manual* (Moody's Investor Service, Inc.); *Dun's Million Dollar Directory* (Dun & Bradstreet); *Thomas Register* (Thomas Publishing Company); and *Standard & Poors Register of Corporations, Directors and Executives* (Standard & Poors Corporation).

In addition to basic library research, you should explore other ready sources of information. Two excellent sources are television and radio. Look at program listings for news, magazines, and special programs which report on contemporary business events. Explore local, regional, or national coverage. Don't be afraid to try to contact someone you heard on such a program. If they, or their secretary, might help you gain more information on a topic of interest, contact them.

Another important source of information that is becoming increasingly effective is the computerized **database**. Almost every kind of information previously available only in hard copy can now be accessed through personal computers. Computers can save you a lot of valuable time and they are easy to use. However, it may also be expensive to use one, depending upon the hourly rate for the database you wish to use. Check your local libraries. Many of them now have PCs and excellent databases available to the public.

Databases are available through database vendors. You will find them advertised in various computer or data processing publications. To access databases on businesses and careers, consult *How to Look It Up On-line* by Alfred Glossbrenner (New York: St. Martin's Press, 1987). Additional directories are listed in Appendix A.

Often, the best source of information is people who work in the career or occupational areas which interest you. Learn as much as you can from them about the opportunities, the challenges, the frustrations, and the potential in that area. Each source you use in exploring the market should be documented. Keep notes on all of the information you obtain about opportunities as you do your research.

Even the conversations you have with different people should be noted and documented. These people may be helpful to you later. You will want to refer back to them and use them as additional resources. Be sure to ask anyone you speak with regarding career opportunities if they know of anybody else that would be helpful for you to speak with. A second or third referral may be much more informative than the original contact.

In addition to consulting business publications, professional publications, databases, and knowledgeable people, keep checking the basic sources which list openings. Newspapers, journals, **job banks**, personnel firms, network contacts, state agencies, and job posting systems (openly published and updated through personnel offices, etc.), are examples. These should be part of your research even though you may not intend to apply for those listings now. Unfortunately, many people go right to those sources immediately without taking the time to explore the market carefully first. These people may never identify areas that offer the most potential. Therefore, you should first become familiar with job postings and different listing vehicles so you can gain insight on the market

for your skills before you apply for a position. Of course,
if something unusually attractive appears to be available
through one of the basic sources, it is wise to investigate
it closely.

Market Exploration Activities

1. First, develop a general career focus that will help you
    guide your research efforts. For example, identify
    private vs. public sector, large vs. small organizations,
    geographic preference, type of industry, level of income
    desired, personal and family considerations, etc.

2. Define the specific type of career opportunities you are
    most interested in pursuing. This definition should
    include not only the skill areas but examples of types
    of positions which require these skills.

3. List the specific criteria for assessing the market,
    industries, and organizations that are important to
    you. Examples may include upward mobility, potential
    for increased earnings, flexibility in other career direc-
    tions, opportunity for decision making, rewards, etc.

4. Identify the formal sources of market exploration such
    as professional associations, business libraries and
    published sources of information that you intend to
    use and make sure you do your research.

5. Identify resource personnel that you may contact and
    use to help you explore the market. Document what
    you learn from each source. Keep this information
    for later use (when you actually pursue new job
    opportunities).

6.   Identify the basic sources of information regarding
     openings. These include newspaper ads, job banks,
     personnel firms, etc. They will help you identify poten-
     tial opportunities in your areas of interest. Look at the
     demand trends they indicate as well as the openings for
     which you will be best suited once you begin your
     formal job search.

Questions for Review

1. What are three basic reference directories important in your research?

2. Other than libraries, what other sources of information are helpful in the research process?

3. What is the objective in exploring the market?

4. What five steps would you use in exploring the job market and identifying job opportunities?

5. What information should you obtain when contacting individuals currently working in your field of interest?

Chapter Six:

Resume Development and Preparation

In a man's letter his soul lies naked.
                Samual Johnson

Your Resume is a Tool

Your resume is an important tool. With careful development, it can help you market yourself to a potential employer. A resume is a sales tool as well as a factual document—it represents you in your absence. It may be the most important communication you will write in the process of career transition. However, many people put so much effort into writing a resume, that they overestimate the power of a resume. They think it can do the promotional job for them. Don't fall into this trap. Your resume is a valuable tool, but it cannot get you the job all on its own.

Your resume's ability to work for or against you depends upon its **communicative power** and its **credibility**. If your resume is not concise and visually appealing, it will not attract the appropriate attention to your qualifications. Usually, resumes are scanned quickly the first time someone looks at them. Your resume must be powerful enough to communicate your experience during this quick scan. If it lacks this power, the reader may overlook some important part of your credentials. Creating a powerful resume is an art. It must be designed to attract attention, yet it also must be factual and believable. For your resume to be credible, you must be able to support the information in it. Your resume projects an image. You must be able to live up to that image if you want someone to hire you.

The Benefits of Writing a Resume

The primary function of your resume is to list your experience and credentials, yet it serves several other functions too. Writing a resume forces you to focus upon the direction you want your career to take. Once you decide which types of career opportunities you wish to pursue, you will be able to determine what experience and credentials to include on your resume. Furthermore, writing your resume will help you recognize your assets. Knowing your strengths and referring to them in your interviews will strengthen your presentation.

Your resume supplements regular job applications. It often lists and emphasizes information not included on the application. Furthermore, it remains as a permanent part of employer records for additional opportunities that may not have been open when you originally applied.

Your resume also can help you network. Place it in the hands of each reference and network contact who may be interested in helping you. A well-written resume will help them refer to your strengths and abilities as they speak to others about you.

Resume Formats—Which Should You Use?

There are three basic formats for resumes: chronological; functional; and combination. A **chronological format** is the traditional format. In it, experience, education, and achievements are detailed in the order in which they were acquired. The **functional format** is a summary of a person's basic skills and experience. Specific dates associated with each skill or position are not usually listed in this format. The **combination format** combines aspects from both styles. This type of format usually includes an emphasis on function and experience, but may include start and stop dates for specific positions in a summary following the experience section. See Table 6-1 to find out which format is best for you.

RESUME TYPE	DESCRIPTION	ADVANTAGES	DISADVANTAGES	BEST USE
Chronological	Most commonly used. Experience is presented in reverse chronological order including job title, company name, dates of employment and a brief description of duties.	Easy to read. Most familiar style used. Easy to organize and write. Allows concise and direct presen-tation of the facts.	Any employment gaps (periods in which you were unemployed) will be obvious.	It has the most universal applica-tion of the various resume types. It can be used for all types of professions and occupations.
Functional	Focus is upon describing skill and experience areas in general or non-specific contexts. Emphasis is upon what you did, not when, how long, or for whom.	Allows you to spotlight key activities or skills you believe need to be emphasized. It can also help you conceal employment gaps or short employ-ment periods.	This type of resume may appear to be more hype than con-tent. Many employers may be skeptical of it because it is often used to hide employ-ment gaps or short tenure with employers.	Highlighting and emphasizing key experience; hiding employment gaps or short tenure with employers.
Combination— Chronological/ Functional	Combines advan-tages of the other two. Begins with a functional ap-proach to empha-size important experience. Provides more detailed descrip-tion of employers, job titles and dates after functional section, though much more limited than a chronologi-cal resume	Allows you to emphasize areas you believe are most important, while allowing you to provide details regarding your specific employ-ment periods.	May be a little confusing to the reader because many of the specific details of the activities listed in the functional section are not described there.	People with limited experience or those desiring to de-emphasize employ-ment gaps or short tenure with certain employers.

Table 6-1: Resume Formats

CAROLYN SMALL
1234 East Haster Place
Englewood, CO 80112
(303) 555-5346

PROFESSIONAL EXPERIENCE

ABC, Inc., Denver, CO 1981-1990

Land Representative, Land Department (1986-1990)
- Negotiated and prepared drilling agreements, oil field equipment contracts, gas balancing contracts, real estate leases and resolutions of disputes between Company, royalty owners and joint venture partners. Represented Company in debt collection matters involving foreign and domestic corporations.
- Negotiated and closed transactions for the sale and purchase of producing oil and gas fields worth several million in revenue.

Contract Administrator, Land Department (1981-1986)
- Supervised staff of six analysts in administration of oil/gas and mineral leases covering 3.5 million acres of land located in 29 states. Approved payments of rental and shut-in royalty totalling $8 million/year.
- Managed successful conversion of computerized records involving 28,000 properties during acquisition of major oil company. Carried discretionary authority to maintain or discontinue selective company operations. Approved title prior to drilling of development and exploratory wells.
- Trained professional staff and established organizational structure to promote efficient work flow. Hired personnel, created job descriptions and conducted employee performance reviews.

Internal Revenue Service, Bismarck, ND and Denver, CO 1979-1981

Tax Attorney
- Represented government in estate and gift tax cases to assure compliance with federal tax statutes and regulations.
- Analyzed business accounting practices and financial statement to determine value of businesses for estate tax purposes. Gained extensive experience in business and real estate valuation.

EDUCATION
J.D., University of North Dakota, 1978. Admitted to practice in North Dakota, 1978.
University of Alaska, 1974-1975, 17 hours toward M.A., Public Administration
B.A., Political Science, Montana State University, 1973.

ALLAN G. SPENCER
123 Sycamore Street
Birmingham, OH 48009
Home (313) 555-0707
Office: (313) 555-5910

BACKGROUND SUMMARY

Extensive, in-depth experience in all phases of personnel with emphasis on compensation, benefits, and international administration. Highly people-skilled manager adept at bringing together and utilizing diverse people in multi-disciplined approach to problem solving and procedural implementation.

PROFESSIONAL ACCOMPLISHMENTS

COMPENSATION

- Formed and led multi-disciplinary task force to develop and implement new concept for merit review process which substitute midpoint with "market range" and created performance level definitions emphasizing "continuous improvement."

- Directed task force which designed new in-house computerized records system, providing more data with greater flexibility and proper documentation.

- Managed the assimilation of salaried positions of newly acquired companies into company-wide salary structure. Developed rational approach to position people properly in range.

- Developed new compensation philosophy and salary structure for Director General, Mexico, to reduce turnover by becoming "above average" payor. Initiated discussions with corporate and group executives and received approval to implement.

- Initiated discussions with senior management on salary review for Mexican subsidiaries. Developed program for pre-approval of annual compensation plan, enhancing local control over budgets and timeliness of reviews.

- Directed joint effort of MIS and users in selecting software to update computerized employe records system. New system had more data with greater flexibility and allowed non-technical people to program.

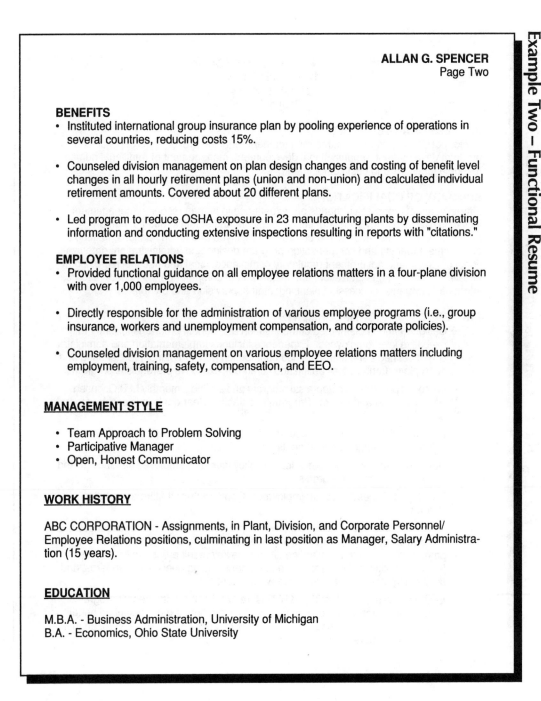

ALLAN G. SPENCER
Page Two

BENEFITS
- Instituted international group insurance plan by pooling experience of operations in several countries, reducing costs 15%.

- Counseled division management on plan design changes and costing of benefit level changes in all hourly retirement plans (union and non-union) and calculated individual retirement amounts. Covered about 20 different plans.

- Led program to reduce OSHA exposure in 23 manufacturing plants by disseminating information and conducting extensive inspections resulting in reports with "citations."

EMPLOYEE RELATIONS
- Provided functional guidance on all employee relations matters in a four-plane division with over 1,000 employees.

- Directly responsible for the administration of various employee programs (i.e., group insurance, workers and unemployment compensation, and corporate policies).

- Counseled division management on various employee relations matters including employment, training, safety, compensation, and EEO.

MANAGEMENT STYLE

- Team Approach to Problem Solving
- Participative Manager
- Open, Honest Communicator

WORK HISTORY

ABC CORPORATION - Assignments, in Plant, Division, and Corporate Personnel/ Employee Relations positions, culminating in last position as Manager, Salary Administration (15 years).

EDUCATION

M.B.A. - Business Administration, University of Michigan
B.A. - Economics, Ohio State University

RALPH WASHINGTON
1234 Bryant Parkway
Lansing, Michigan 48341
(313) 555-6430

PROFESSIONAL OBJECTIVE
Senior position in human resource management requiring proven skills in policy and program development, organizational development, management of traditional human resource functions and cost containment.

SUMMARY OF QUALIFICATIONS
Fifteen years of progressive "hands on" experience in human resource management including experience in: planning, implementation, and administration of human resource policies, procedures and programs; employee and union relations; training and development; benefit and compensation program design and administration; organizational development; government regulatory compliance; local and national recruiting at all levels; selection, customization, and installation of computer based human resource information systems; succession planning; staff supervision and payroll.

PROFESSIONAL ACCOMPLISHMENTS
- Designed and implemented compensation and benefit programs for entry to executive level employees. Experience includes implementation and administration of defined benefit and defined contribution pension plans, profit sharing and 401K plans, bonus, stock option and numerous executive prerequisite programs.

- Improved performance appraisal program and started a monthly M.B.O. based Work Planning and Review Program to establish clear goals in line with corporate objectives.

- Established the first human resource department in four organizations, in both union and non-union environments.

- Developed and wrote human resource policy manuals, employee handbooks, and employee orientation programs.

- Developed successful Equal Employment Opportunity and Affirmative Action Programs.

- Developed and conducted productivity improvement programs for executive and senior management. Programs focused on: defining the positions/business units primary function and mission, identifying the key result areas - critical success factors, identifying the areas of measurement, setting goals and standards, and developing measurement and review methods.

- Evaluated, redesigned, and had bid insured and self-funded benefit programs resulting in faster claim service, easier administration, a more balanced benefit program, and lowered insurance premiums by 26%. At two employers, annual savings were more than $100,000.

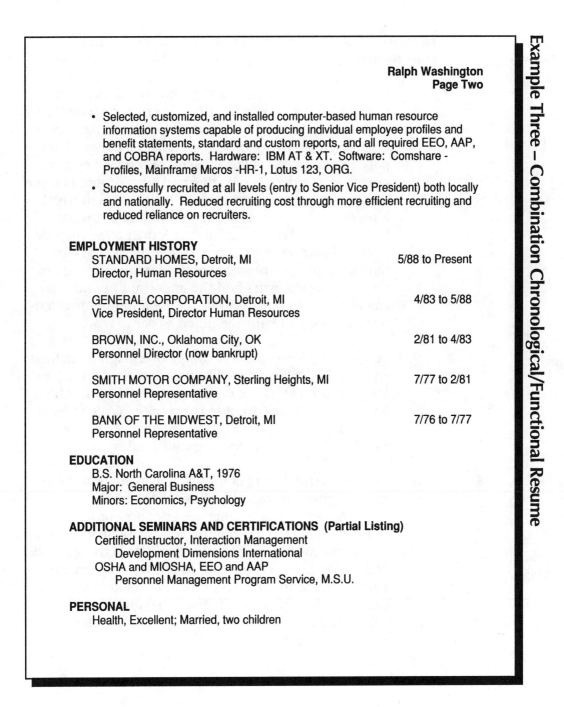

Ralph Washington
Page Two

- Selected, customized, and installed computer-based human resource information systems capable of producing individual employee profiles and benefit statements, standard and custom reports, and all required EEO, AAP, and COBRA reports. Hardware: IBM AT & XT. Software: Comshare - Profiles, Mainframe Micros -HR-1, Lotus 123, ORG.

- Successfully recruited at all levels (entry to Senior Vice President) both locally and nationally. Reduced recruiting cost through more efficient recruiting and reduced reliance on recruiters.

EMPLOYMENT HISTORY

STANDARD HOMES, Detroit, MI Director, Human Resources	5/88 to Present
GENERAL CORPORATION, Detroit, MI Vice President, Director Human Resources	4/83 to 5/88
BROWN, INC., Oklahoma City, OK Personnel Director (now bankrupt)	2/81 to 4/83
SMITH MOTOR COMPANY, Sterling Heights, MI Personnel Representative	7/77 to 2/81
BANK OF THE MIDWEST, Detroit, MI Personnel Representative	7/76 to 7/77

EDUCATION
B.S. North Carolina A&T, 1976
Major: General Business
Minors: Economics, Psychology

ADDITIONAL SEMINARS AND CERTIFICATIONS (Partial Listing)
Certified Instructor, Interaction Management
     Development Dimensions International
OSHA and MIOSHA, EEO and AAP
     Personnel Management Program Service, M.S.U.

PERSONAL
Health, Excellent; Married, two children

Here are a few basic guidelines to follow when writing
your resume.

1.   When writing a resume, use as few words as possible
     to provide complete facts. Keep the resume **concise** by
     avoiding repetition and too much detail. In most cases,
     a resume should not be longer than two pages. A one-
     page resume is usually sufficient for a recent college
     graduate or a person who has had a maximum of three
     distinct job titles. There may be some cases in which
     a person's experience simply will not fit on two pages.
     In that case, of course, a third or fourth page must be
     added. However, keep in mind that the people who
     read your resume probably have to read many others
     too. If he or she can't find the important information
     easily, your resume may not get the appropriate atten-
     tion. A concise resume is much easier to read.

2.   Make sure your resume is complete enough to include
     your most significant qualifications without dwelling on
     insignificant details. Your strongest credentials should
     be immediately apparent to the reader. Write at least
     two rough versions and get others to read and com-
     ment on them before drafting your final version.

3.   The **aesthetic** appeal of the resume is important too.
     An attractive resume will influence the reader in a
     positive way. If the resume does not appear to be a
     first-class effort, it will not make a favorable impression
     upon the reader. Try to make good use of the space on
     each page, but don't attempt to use up the extra space
     with insignificant or inaccurate information. Instead,
     use the white space on the pages to your advantage.
     Adjust the layout to make your resume pleasing to look
     at and easy to read.

4. Avoid overstatement and **embellishment**. Your resume will be at its best if it provides important facts in a concise and direct manner without attempting to inflate your achievements. People who screen resumes have seen thousands of them and are sensitive to fact versus fiction.

5. Make no assumptions about the reader's knowledge of your area of expertise. Write the resume in a way that almost any reader will understand. Avoid using technical terms unless the situation requires it; even then, use the simplest terms possible.

Elements of the Resume

All resumes include the same basic elements (heading, objective, employment experience, education, activities, and accomplishments). The elements must be developed using three guidelines. First, the information must be absolutely necessary. Second, the information must provide a positive view of your qualifications. Third, the information must be factual.

Begin the resume with the data that tells people who you are. This is the **Heading**. This includes your name, address, and telephone number. Put this information at the top of the first page. You do not need to label the document "resume." If your resume is longer than one page, you will want to add your name (and maybe your phone number) to the top of the additional pages as well. Usually, the information is centered on the first page, and appears in the upper right corner on the following pages.

Many experts on resume writing encourage you to include a **Career Objective** after the personal information. However, a written objective can be risky unless you are careful. If you write it with a specific focus, it may screen out some opportunities for which you would like to be considered. If it is too general, you risk making an ambiguous statement that means nothing and reflects poorly upon you.

If you choose to include a career objective, either make it fairly general, to cover a variety of positions that might interest you; or, create several different versions of your resume with different specific career objectives. Different versions of your resume will require you to be more thorough in your record-keeping, but they may be a real advantage to you.

Your **Employment Experience** should come next. This is the most important part of the resume because it summarizes your qualifications. It is here that the three resume formats differ. The chronological format is generally the best way to present your experience, because it is usually the easiest format for the reader to comprehend. To use this format, list each of the significant jobs or positions you have held with the beginning and termination dates for each. Begin with the most recent position and work back. State the month and year in which you started and ended each position. Always include the month whenever possible. If you only include the year, some interviewers may interpret this as an attempt to hide gaps in employment. Of course, if there *is* a lengthy gap in your employment history, it may be to your advantage to include only the years involved.

Functional resumes are designed to focus upon functions, skills, and responsibilities rather than specific positions and time frames. By emphasizing your functions, you can spot-light specific experiences. However, this often leaves out important information such as when you performed the function, how long you did it, and how it integrates with the rest of your experience. The functional resume, by its nature, hides certain information. It can be useful to people who wish to cover significant employment gaps or frequent job changes.

To highlight your functional experience, you should consider using a combination chronological/functional resume. See Example Three. This format includes the time frames associated with your work history. If you choose this format, read it over carefully to make sure you haven't unintentionally overinflated your qualifications.

When writing any resume, you must decide whether you will choose a general or targeted approach. A **general approach** does not emphasize a specific area of experience or interest. In it, you provide all of your career experience and skills without highlighting skills appropriate for a specific career objective. A general approach is suitable for people who are open to several different types of positions.

A **targeted approach** involves a specific objective keyed to a particular type of position. This type of resume emphasizes all of your experience that relates directly to that type of position. A targeted resume is appropriate for people who seek a specific type of position, and who possess skills that will be required for that position. Example Four shows a resume with a targeted approach.

Example Four– Targeted Approach

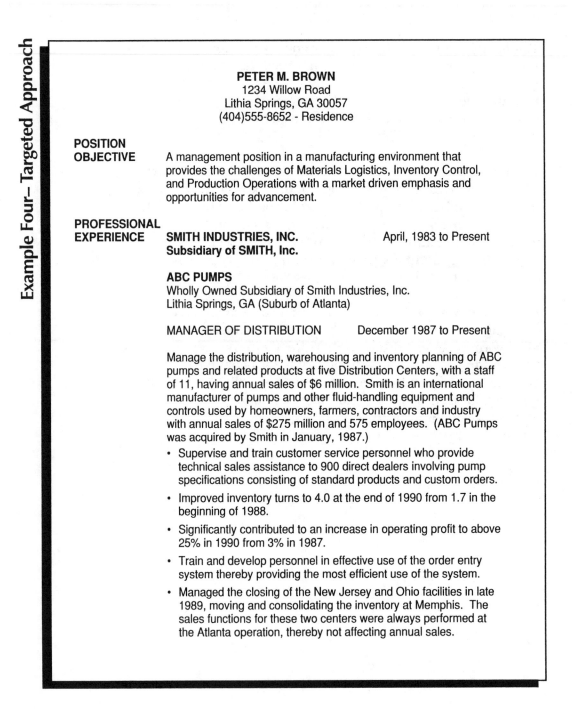

PETER M. BROWN
1234 Willow Road
Lithia Springs, GA 30057
(404)555-8652 - Residence

**POSITION
OBJECTIVE**   A management position in a manufacturing environment that
provides the challenges of Materials Logistics, Inventory Control,
and Production Operations with a market driven emphasis and
opportunities for advancement.

**PROFESSIONAL
EXPERIENCE**   **SMITH INDUSTRIES, INC.**   April, 1983 to Present
Subsidiary of SMITH, Inc.

ABC PUMPS
Wholly Owned Subsidiary of Smith Industries, Inc.
Lithia Springs, GA (Suburb of Atlanta)

MANAGER OF DISTRIBUTION   December 1987 to Present

Manage the distribution, warehousing and inventory planning of ABC
pumps and related products at five Distribution Centers, with a staff
of 11, having annual sales of $6 million. Smith is an international
manufacturer of pumps and other fluid-handling equipment and
controls used by homeowners, farmers, contractors and industry
with annual sales of $275 million and 575 employees. (ABC Pumps
was acquired by Smith in January, 1987.)

• Supervise and train customer service personnel who provide
  technical sales assistance to 900 direct dealers involving pump
  specifications consisting of standard products and custom orders.

• Improved inventory turns to 4.0 at the end of 1990 from 1.7 in the
  beginning of 1988.

• Significantly contributed to an increase in operating profit to above
  25% in 1990 from 3% in 1987.

• Train and develop personnel in effective use of the order entry
  system thereby providing the most efficient use of the system.

• Managed the closing of the New Jersey and Ohio facilities in late
  1989, moving and consolidating the inventory at Memphis. The
  sales functions for these two centers were always performed at
  the Atlanta operation, thereby not affecting annual sales.

PETER M. BROWN
Page Two

SMITH INDUSTRIES, INC.
ABC SYSTEMS GROUP
Union City, TN

PURCHASING MANAGER   April 1983 to December 1987

Accountable for the sourcing decisions, planning, ordering and follow-up of all purchased items amounting to $12 million annually for this manufacturing facility producing swimming pool filters, agriculture and industrial pumps and drainers.
- Established basic forecasting and material requirements procedures.
- Consolidated manufacturing and inventory into existing operations from two acquisitions in 1985 (Swimequip, El Paso) and a part of Flowtec (Dayton) in 1986.
- Achieved a 2% reduction in end unit material cost in 1985, compared to a 1984 1.6% reduction in 1986 during consolidation.

JONES, INC.   February 1968 to March 1983

A manufacturer of agricultural tractors and farm implements with plants in 27 countries including three in the U.S. (Akron, Des Moines, and Detroit). The holding company, in Toronto, CAN is #1 in tractor sales worldwide, with $1.2 billion in annual sales.

PRODUCTION CONTROL MANAGER   May 1981 to March 1983
Akron, OH

Established and maintained the department and procedures to effectively control timely delivery of outgoing products with the least practical inventory and manpower for this start-up operation manufacturing industrial and construction machinery.
- Supervised Metal Control, Programming, Shop Scheduling, Material Handling and Pre-Production Control involving 31 salaried and 42 hourly employees.
- Managed an average inventory of $9 million, which included the importing of 34% of material dollars input from Italy and Germany consisting of Dozer and Excavator chassis.

Example Four – Targeted Approach

PETER M. BROWN
Page Three

MARKETING SPECIFICATION   April 1977 to May 1981
MANAGER
Des Moines, IA

- Managed a project to install an improved product coding
  approach that provided field sales with a clear and precise
  tracking system.

PRODUCTION CONTROL   January 1970 to April 1977
MANAGER
Detroit, MI

- Planned, provisioned, and controlled production of tractors at a
  rate of 150 to 175 daily, supervising 44 salaried and 51 hourly
  employees.

INVENTORY ANALYST,   February 1968 to January 1970
EXPEDITOR &
PRODUCTION PLANNER
Detroit, MI

EDUCATION   B.S. Business Administration
                  Pennsylvania State University, December, 1967

HOBBIES   Private flying, fishing, and occasional golf.

PERSONAL   Excellent health, married, five grown children, willing to travel
                  and relocate.

REFERENCES   Furnished when a mutual interest has been established.

As you develop the employment history section of your resume, remember that the information you include must be necessary, positive, and factual. Also, remember to be as direct and concise as possible. A problem many people have is deciding how much information is necessary and how much information is *too* much. To help you decide what information to include, write a brief job description for each position you will list before writing the resume. Your brief job description should include the title, a sentence or two describing the goal of the job, and four to eight specific duties or activities. You are not actually going to transfer all of this to your resume; but this will help you organize the information before deciding how you will include it.

Once you have a brief job description for each position, go back and prioritize the specific duties you performed. If you are writing a targeted resume, you will want to choose those duties or activities that most relate to the area for which you are applying. You may not have room to list all the facets of each job on your resume. Remember—be concise.

You can choose from three different methods to describe the various stages of your career. The **global** method uses one or two paragraphs to describe each job. See Example Five. The paragraphs should explain the nature of your position and the responsibilities and skills that were required to fulfill you duties. The **outline** method requires you to capture the essence of the position in short, direct statements. See Example Six. It allows the reader to scan the resume more quickly. The **task specific** method is similar to the outline, but provides more detail. It combines the advantage of a global statement for each job with highlights of your duties and achievements. These highlights are more detailed than in the outline format. See Example Seven. If you plan to apply to positions in more than one field, you should develop a resume that provides the appropriate emphasis on your qualifications for each field.

ELAINE G. MILLER
123 Spring Hollow
Napier, Illinois 50881
Home: (312) 555-2548
Office: (312) 555-5910

OBJECTIVE

Senior level compensation management position emphasizing challenge and real contribution to corporate objectives.

BACKGROUND SUMMARY

Extensive, in-depth experience in all phases of personnel with emphasis on compensation, benefits, and international administration. Highly people-skilled manager adept at bringing together and utilizing diverse people in multi-disciplined approach to problem solving and procedural implementation.

PROFESSIONAL ACCOMPLISHMENTS

COMPENSATION (Domestic and International)
- Counseled policy committee on yearly compensation plan for all domestic business units affecting approximately 3,000 salaried employees. Received approval on recommended course of action.
- Directed multi-disciplined effort which reduced number of exempt salary grades by 50% and created more structure in job evaluation. Same concept extended to non-exempt structures on selective basis.
- Formed and led multi-disciplinary task force to develop and implement new concept for merit review process which substituted midpoint with "market range" and created performance level definitions emphasizing "continuous improvement."
- Directed task force which designed new in-house computerized records system, providing more data with greater flexibility and proper documentation.
- Managed the assimilation of salaried positions of newly acquired companies into company-wide salary structure. Developed rational approach to position people properly in range.

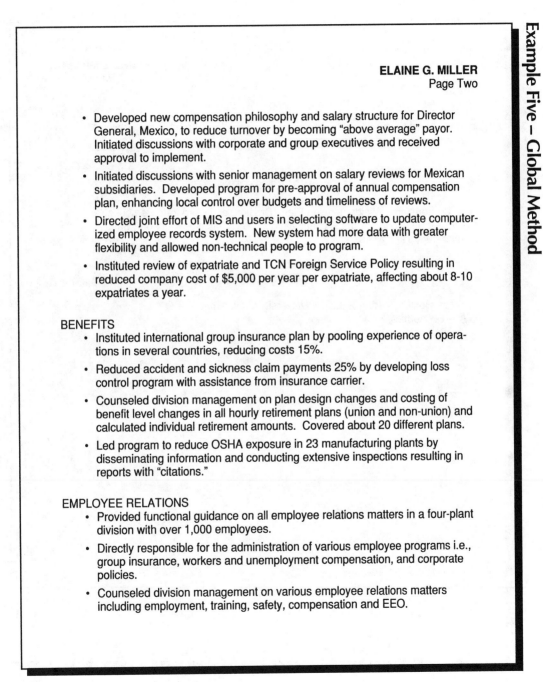

ELAINE G. MILLER
Page Two

- Developed new compensation philosophy and salary structure for Director General, Mexico, to reduce turnover by becoming "above average" payor. Initiated discussions with corporate and group executives and received approval to implement.

- Initiated discussions with senior management on salary reviews for Mexican subsidiaries. Developed program for pre-approval of annual compensation plan, enhancing local control over budgets and timeliness of reviews.

- Directed joint effort of MIS and users in selecting software to update computerized employee records system. New system had more data with greater flexibility and allowed non-technical people to program.

- Instituted review of expatriate and TCN Foreign Service Policy resulting in reduced company cost of $5,000 per year per expatriate, affecting about 8-10 expatriates a year.

BENEFITS
- Instituted international group insurance plan by pooling experience of operations in several countries, reducing costs 15%.

- Reduced accident and sickness claim payments 25% by developing loss control program with assistance from insurance carrier.

- Counseled division management on plan design changes and costing of benefit level changes in all hourly retirement plans (union and non-union) and calculated individual retirement amounts. Covered about 20 different plans.

- Led program to reduce OSHA exposure in 23 manufacturing plants by disseminating information and conducting extensive inspections resulting in reports with "citations."

EMPLOYEE RELATIONS
- Provided functional guidance on all employee relations matters in a four-plant division with over 1,000 employees.

- Directly responsible for the administration of various employee programs i.e., group insurance, workers and unemployment compensation, and corporate policies.

- Counseled division management on various employee relations matters including employment, training, safety, compensation and EEO.

Example Five – Global Method

ELAINE G. MILLER
Page Three

MANAGEMENT STYLE
* Team approach to Problem Solving
* Participative Manager
* Open. Honest Communicator

WORK HISTORY

ABC Corporation – Assignments in Plant, Division, and Corporate Personnel/ Employee Relations positions, culminating in last position as Manager, Salary Administration (15 years).

EDUCATION

M.B.A. – Business Administration, University of Michigan
B.A. – Economics, Harvard College

TIM JONES
1234 Cold Spring Lane
Avalon, Pennsylvania
(313) 555-1234

OBJECTIVE
Senior position in human resource management requiring proven skills in policy and program development, organizational development, management of traditional human resource functions and cost containment.

SUMMARY OF QUALIFICATIONS
Thirteen years of progressive "hands on" experience in human resource management including experience in: planning, implementation, and administration of human resource policies, procedures and programs; employee and union relations; training and development; benefit and compensation program design and administration; organizational development; government regulatory compliance; local and national recruiting at all levels; selection, customization, and installation of computer based human resource information systems; succession planning; staff supervision and payroll.

PROFESSIONAL ACCOMPLISHMENTS
- Established the first human resource department in four organizations, in both union and non-union environments.

- Developed and wrote H.R. policy manuals, employee handbooks, and employee orientation programs.

- Developed successful Equal Employment Opportunity and Affirmative Action Programs.

- Designed and implemented compensation and benefit programs for entry to executive level employees. Experience includes implementation and administration of defined benefit and defined contribution pension plans, profit sharing and 401K plans, bonus, stock option and numerous executive perquisite programs.

- Improved performance appraisal program and started a monthly M.B.O. based Work Planning and Review Program to establish clear goals in line with corporate objectives.

- Developed and conducted productivity improvement programs for executive and senior management. Programs focused on: defining the positions/business units primary function and mission, identifying the key result areas - critical success factors, identifying the areas of measurement, setting goals and standards, and developing measurement and review methods.

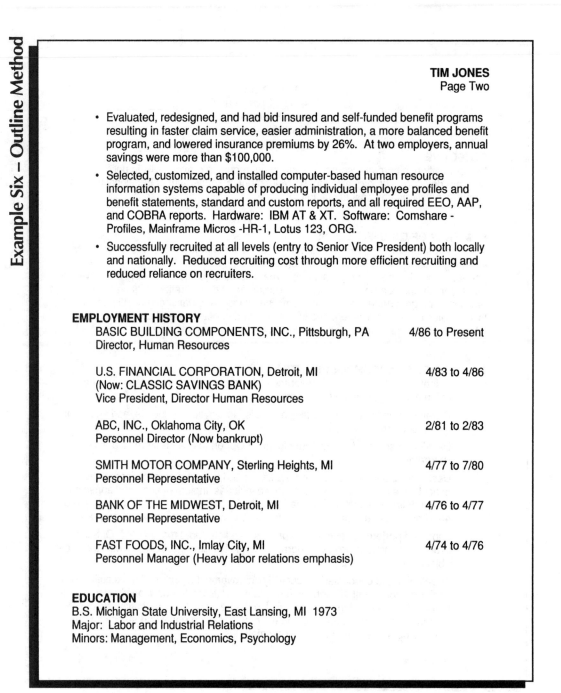

Example Six – Outline Method

TIM JONES
Page Two

- Evaluated, redesigned, and had bid insured and self-funded benefit programs resulting in faster claim service, easier administration, a more balanced benefit program, and lowered insurance premiums by 26%. At two employers, annual savings were more than $100,000.

- Selected, customized, and installed computer-based human resource information systems capable of producing individual employee profiles and benefit statements, standard and custom reports, and all required EEO, AAP, and COBRA reports. Hardware: IBM AT & XT. Software: Comshare - Profiles, Mainframe Micros -HR-1, Lotus 123, ORG.

- Successfully recruited at all levels (entry to Senior Vice President) both locally and nationally. Reduced recruiting cost through more efficient recruiting and reduced reliance on recruiters.

EMPLOYMENT HISTORY

BASIC BUILDING COMPONENTS, INC., Pittsburgh, PA   4/86 to Present
Director, Human Resources

U.S. FINANCIAL CORPORATION, Detroit, MI   4/83 to 4/86
(Now: CLASSIC SAVINGS BANK)
Vice President, Director Human Resources

ABC, INC., Oklahoma City, OK   2/81 to 2/83
Personnel Director (Now bankrupt)

SMITH MOTOR COMPANY, Sterling Heights, MI   4/77 to 7/80
Personnel Representative

BANK OF THE MIDWEST, Detroit, MI   4/76 to 4/77
Personnel Representative

FAST FOODS, INC., Imlay City, MI   4/74 to 4/76
Personnel Manager (Heavy labor relations emphasis)

EDUCATION
B.S. Michigan State University, East Lansing, MI 1973
Major: Labor and Industrial Relations
Minors: Management, Economics, Psychology

TIM JONES
Page Three

Completed 27 graduate credits, School of Labor and Industrial Relations, Michigan State University

ADDITIONAL SEMINARS AND CERTIFICATIONS (Partial Listing)
Certified Instructor, Interaction Management
   Development Dimensions International
Pension Plan Design and Administration, Assessment Centers, Employee Handbook and Policy Manual Development, Labor and Employment Law Updates
   Employers Association of Detroit
OSHA and MIOSHA, EEO and AAP
   Personnel Management Program Service, M.S.U.

PERSONAL
Health, Excellent; Single; Willing to Travel

ERIC STALLINGS, C.P.M.
1234 Wheaton Oaks Drive
Wheaton, Illinois 60187
(312) 555-0481

JOB OBJECTIVE
<u>Senior Purchasing Managerial position</u> with a large manufacturing company seeking an individual with value analysis, cost reduction, foreign and domestic sourcing, contract negotiation/ administration, program management and JIT experience.

EXPERIENCE

1989-Present   <u>ABC ELECTRIC SUPPLY</u>, Elmhurst, Illinois.

<u>Foreign Sourcing Manager</u>. Report to Manager, Inventory and Purchasing. Direct 2 managers with 8 buyers and one clerical subordinate. Responsible for offshore procurement program and all non-GE product purchases for this $1,200,000,000 business. Function includes areas of purchasing analysis, inventory management, supplier sourcing, and vendor consolidation.

- Reduced vendor base for specific commodity to lower cost and standardize product. Achieved $75,000 annualized savings.

1987-1989   <u>SMITH-BROWN MOTORS</u>
Bloomington, Illinois.

<u>Purchasing Coordinator</u>. Reported to Manager, Production Purchasing. Responsible for annual production parts purchases exceeding $200,000,000 and for additional $18,000,000 in tooling. Duties included supplier evaluation, JIT inventory management, pricing analysis, cost reduction, and interface with Engineering and Quality Control to ensure specifications compliance.

- Led team of department coordinators to analyze 20 suppliers' capabilities in addition to negotiating pricing and delivery requirements. Achieved assured delivery of defect free components in timely manner, and reduced cost by over $100,000.

ERIC STALLINGS, C.P.M.
Page Two

- Negotiated sequential components delivery to production line to supersede in-house production plan. Savings obtained in equipment acquisition costs and reduced production line head count, while achieving acquisition cost 5% below standard. Total program savings exceeded $750,000.

- Together with Tool Engineer, I challenged $1,200,000 bill for tools to produce major component. Analysis of supplier's cost, post delivery, demonstrated unjustified inclusion of capital equipment with corresponding $200,000 price adjustment.

1981-1987 ABC LABORATORIES, Deerfield, Illinois.

Senior Capital Equipment Buyer-Corporate. Reported to Purchasing Manager-Capital Equipment. Responsible for complete acquisition of major capital equipment for 4 domestic and 2 offshore operations, and for coordinating with Engineering to establish performance requirements and equipment specifications for this $5,000,000,000 company. Also drafted consulting agreements for development of custom manufacturing systems, and interacted with Legal to develop standard form equipment contracts.

- Convinced Engineering to modify and utilize technology from another industry to improve efficiency. Received Technical Service Award for verified $1,200,000 annual savings in reduction of head count, scrap, and cycle time.

(1983-1985) Purchasing Manager-Home Therapy Division. Reported to Director of Materials Management. Up to five coordinators, one buyer, and two clericals reported to me. Responsible for design and implementation of systems and procedures to establish purchasing function for new division. Also responsible for coordination with Traffic and Materials Control. Controlled $20,000,000 equipment and materials budget.

- Initiated and conducted feasibility study with Marketing Manager to determine value of entry into durable medical equipment market. Implemented program generated increased sales of $1,250,000 annually.

Example Seven – Task Specific Method

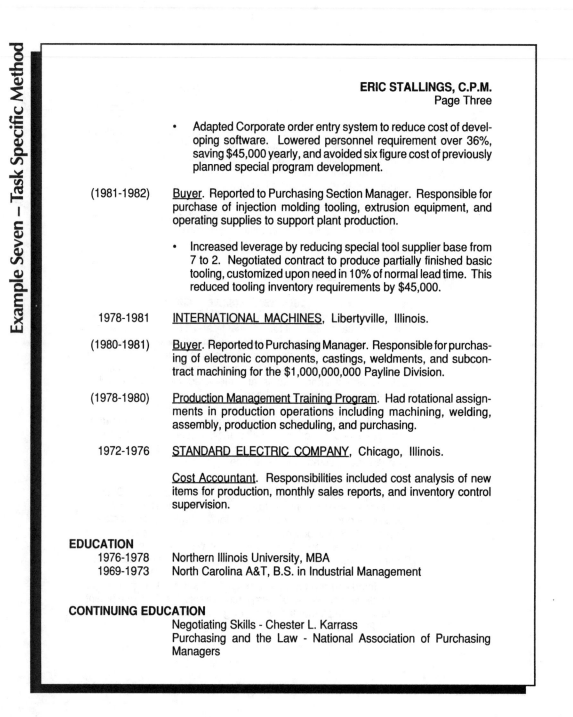

ERIC STALLINGS, C.P.M.
Page Three

- Adapted Corporate order entry system to reduce cost of developing software. Lowered personnel requirement over 36%, saving $45,000 yearly, and avoided six figure cost of previously planned special program development.

(1981-1982)   <u>Buyer</u>. Reported to Purchasing Section Manager. Responsible for purchase of injection molding tooling, extrusion equipment, and operating supplies to support plant production.

- Increased leverage by reducing special tool supplier base from 7 to 2. Negotiated contract to produce partially finished basic tooling, customized upon need in 10% of normal lead time. This reduced tooling inventory requirements by $45,000.

1978-1981   <u>INTERNATIONAL MACHINES</u>, Libertyville, Illinois.

(1980-1981)   <u>Buyer</u>. Reported to Purchasing Manager. Responsible for purchasing of electronic components, castings, weldments, and subcontract machining for the $1,000,000,000 Payline Division.

(1978-1980)   <u>Production Management Training Program</u>. Had rotational assignments in production operations including machining, welding, assembly, production scheduling, and purchasing.

1972-1976   <u>STANDARD ELECTRIC COMPANY</u>, Chicago, Illinois.

<u>Cost Accountant</u>. Responsibilities included cost analysis of new items for production, monthly sales reports, and inventory control supervision.

EDUCATION
1976-1978   Northern Illinois University, MBA
1969-1973   North Carolina A&T, B.S. in Industrial Management

CONTINUING EDUCATION
                Negotiating Skills - Chester L. Karrass
                Purchasing and the Law - National Association of Purchasing Managers

If you are leaving the military to pursue civilian opportunities, be careful to describe your experience in terms that non-military personnel will understand. See Example Eight.

Unless you are a recent college graduate, **Education** should follow your work experience on your resume. This section should include your degrees, certifications, and any other qualifications earned through formal education. See Examples Eight and Nine. For recent college graduates, education is usually placed immediately after the career objective because it is the most recent significant activity in their career path.

JAMES E. KRAMER
1234 Long Meadow Drive
Dayton, Ohio 45432
Home Phone: (513) 555-3258
Business Phone: (513) 555-1027

EDUCATION: MA Public Administration, Central Michigan University, 1985 (3.4 grade point average).

BGE Military & Political Science, University of Nebraska at Omaha, 1974 (2.8 grade point average).

U.S. Air Force Technical Instructor Course, 1979 (Honor Graduate).

EXPERIENCE:

1980-Present   U.S. AIR FORCE, AIR TRAINING COMMAND HEADQUARTERS
(equivalent to Corporate level)

Position: Aircraft Systems Technical Training Project Manager.
Duties: Responsible for the initiation, development and establishment of technical training programs. Insure sufficient qualified instructors, training aids and facilities are available to provide the timely supply of technically proficient personnel to repair and maintain sophisticated aircraft and associated test equipment. Student educational backgrounds varied from grade school through college and foreign students often required English language training or courses taught in their native language. Shared staff supervision of 124,000 personnel and an annual budget of $587.0 million.
Accomplishments: One project to purchase $950,000 in technical training was taken over and reevaluated resulting in acquisition of the training for $700,000. Another project to train 500 non-English speaking persons with eighth grade educations to maintain technically sophisticated avionic systems on several modern aircraft was completed in the unprecedented time of 8 months. Developed and implemented a human relations course which was adopted for use throughout the Department of Defense.

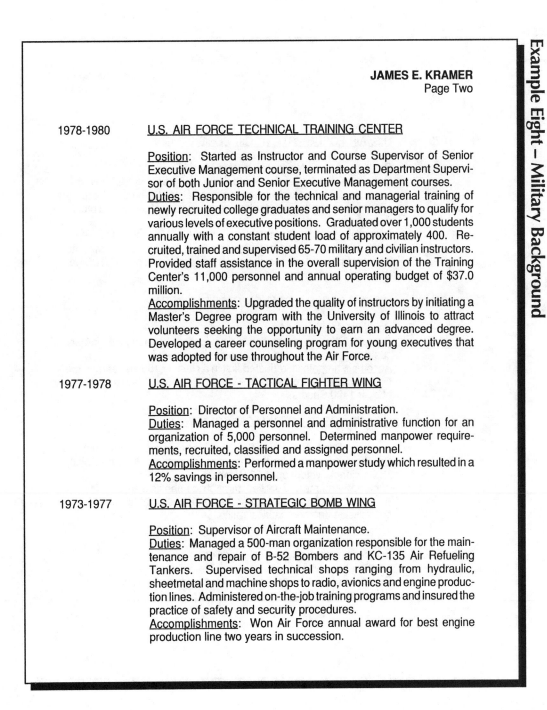

JAMES E. KRAMER
Page Two

1978-1980   U.S. AIR FORCE TECHNICAL TRAINING CENTER

Position: Started as Instructor and Course Supervisor of Senior Executive Management course, terminated as Department Supervisor of both Junior and Senior Executive Management courses.
Duties: Responsible for the technical and managerial training of newly recruited college graduates and senior managers to qualify for various levels of executive positions. Graduated over 1,000 students annually with a constant student load of approximately 400. Recruited, trained and supervised 65-70 military and civilian instructors. Provided staff assistance in the overall supervision of the Training Center's 11,000 personnel and annual operating budget of $37.0 million.
Accomplishments: Upgraded the quality of instructors by initiating a Master's Degree program with the University of Illinois to attract volunteers seeking the opportunity to earn an advanced degree. Developed a career counseling program for young executives that was adopted for use throughout the Air Force.

1977-1978   U.S. AIR FORCE - TACTICAL FIGHTER WING

Position: Director of Personnel and Administration.
Duties: Managed a personnel and administrative function for an organization of 5,000 personnel. Determined manpower requirements, recruited, classified and assigned personnel.
Accomplishments: Performed a manpower study which resulted in a 12% savings in personnel.

1973-1977   U.S. AIR FORCE - STRATEGIC BOMB WING

Position: Supervisor of Aircraft Maintenance.
Duties: Managed a 500-man organization responsible for the maintenance and repair of B-52 Bombers and KC-135 Air Refueling Tankers. Supervised technical shops ranging from hydraulic, sheetmetal and machine shops to radio, avionics and engine production lines. Administered on-the-job training programs and insured the practice of safety and security procedures.
Accomplishments: Won Air Force annual award for best engine production line two years in succession.

Example Eight – Military Background

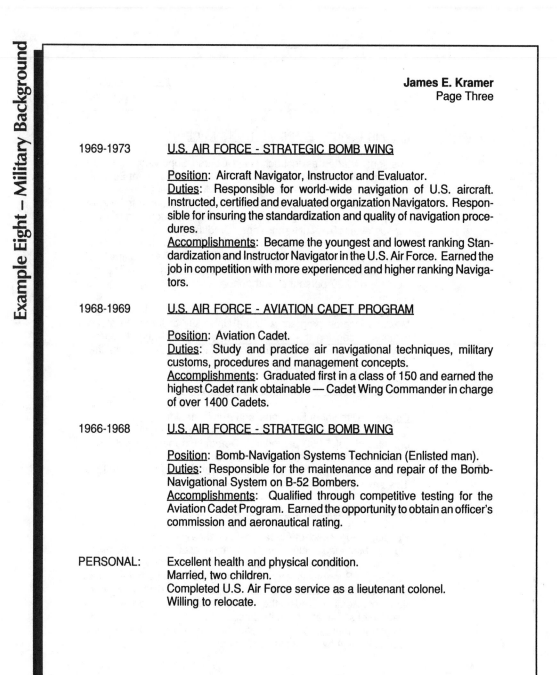

Example Eight – Military Background

James E. Kramer
Page Three

1969-1973   U.S. AIR FORCE - STRATEGIC BOMB WING

Position: Aircraft Navigator, Instructor and Evaluator.
Duties: Responsible for world-wide navigation of U.S. aircraft.
Instructed, certified and evaluated organization Navigators. Responsible for insuring the standardization and quality of navigation procedures.
Accomplishments: Became the youngest and lowest ranking Standardization and Instructor Navigator in the U.S. Air Force. Earned the
job in competition with more experienced and higher ranking Navigators.

1968-1969   U.S. AIR FORCE - AVIATION CADET PROGRAM

Position: Aviation Cadet.
Duties: Study and practice air navigational techniques, military
customs, procedures and management concepts.
Accomplishments: Graduated first in a class of 150 and earned the
highest Cadet rank obtainable — Cadet Wing Commander in charge
of over 1400 Cadets.

1966-1968   U.S. AIR FORCE - STRATEGIC BOMB WING

Position: Bomb-Navigation Systems Technician (Enlisted man).
Duties: Responsible for the maintenance and repair of the Bomb-
Navigational System on B-52 Bombers.
Accomplishments: Qualified through competitive testing for the
Aviation Cadet Program. Earned the opportunity to obtain an officer's
commission and aeronautical rating.

PERSONAL: Excellent health and physical condition.
Married, two children.
Completed U.S. Air Force service as a lieutenant colonel.
Willing to relocate.

The education section of your resume establishes your formal preparation for long-term career success. Always include your degree if you have one. If you graduated with honors or a high grade point average, include these facts too. If there was a particular emphasis in the program, or special courses that you think were particularly important, list them—especially if you are using a targeted resume. See Example Nine.

NANCY TAYLOR
1234 Washington Blvd.
Dearborn, Michigan 48251
(313) 555-1618

WORK EXPERIENCE
November 1988-
Present

ABC Corp., Detroit, Michigan
Collection Department:
Customer Service Representative for retail and lease accounts.
Handle problems or questions that customers encounter on their
accounts, and negotiate payment plans for delinquent customers.

Field Representative:
Performed wholesale audits at dealerships (physical and written).
Personally visit customers to collect payments, arrange for and/or
repossess vehicles.

Cashier:
Process customer receipts, prepare and balance incoming and
outgoing checks, and balance wholesale, and retail ledges. Transmit activity to accounts.

June 1982-
November 1988

Weinhardt's, Rochester, Michigan
Worked in various departments (Women's Sportswear, Jewelry,
and Juniors), restocking merchandise, checking-in merchandise,
working on store displays, and selling store merchandise.

EDUCATION

B.S. Communications, Oakland University, June 1982
Major G.P.A.: 3.3
Related Courses: Technical Writing
                     Economics
                     Computers
                     Speech and Interpersonal Relations

Rochester High School, 1978 College Prep Program
Special Training: Philip Crosby Quality Education Program;
ABC Corp. Quality Education Sessions (designed to plan and
install a process for quality improvement at ABC).

ACTIVITIES

Member of Alpha Chi Omega sorority, Oakland University

REFERENCES

Available upon request.

Some people believe it is necessary to list every program, seminar, or presentation they ever attended. This tends to overinflate your credentials. Or, it may look as if you are trying to lengthen your resume with experience that is not particularly significant. However, if you attended or partici-pated in a program that holds special significance in your educational background, include it.

The inclusion of **Activities and Accomplishments** is a matter of personal choice. It is here that you list awards, accomplishments, or personal or civic achievement activities that you think are worth mentioning. This information is not required, but you may want to include it if it increases your marketability. Ask yourself these questions:

1. Does the activity relate to or show increased capability in my career path?

2. Does the activity show a unique quality or value that increases the chances of my success in a professional capacity?

If the achievement or activity does not clearly support one or both of these goals, you probably should omit it. However, if you are particularly proud of it and you think it reflects your unique nature in some way, go ahead and include it. Just make sure it doesn't clutter the resume.

Some people include a **Personal Data** section on their resumes. If you want to include your interests and hobbies on your resume, you should place them in this section at the end of the resume. Inclusion of this type of information is a matter of personal choice. In making this decision, remember that the people who read your resume are interested in your qualifications for a particular position. If they are interested in learning more about who you are, they can find out in an interview.

Items such as height, weight, age and marital status are no longer mandatory. Do not include them unless the information pertains to the job.

Similarly, some people like to include a photograph of themselves with their resume. Generally, this is not recommended; however, it may work for you. If you choose to do so, don't have your photo printed on your resume. Instead, use a clip-on photo. Some employers are prohibited by law to have employees' pictures in their files. Remember—your resume should promote you on the basis of your experience and qualifications. Unless your appearance somehow qualifies you for the position, you should not allow decisions based upon your appearance to be made until the interview.

References is the final heading on your resume. Most people simply state that references will be furnished upon request. You will undoubtedly be asked for references if you are seriously being considered for a position. There is nothing wrong with listing your references on your resume, but it may be to your advantage to supply them at the interview. This way, you can tell your references more about the nature of the position before your potential employer has a chance to call them. Generally, a list of references should include three professional and three personal contacts to whom your potential employer can refer for information.

Finally, remember that the resume is a document of facts. It should be written in an objective and concise manner. However, it is ultimately a marketing tool designed to create a positive impression of you. Strive to make it look good while remaining truthful about your qualifications and maintaining your objectivity. Your resume will have more credibility if it does not appear to overinflate your credentials. Pay careful attention to the delicate balance between objectivity and marketing in all phases of this project.

Resume Development Tips

1. Pay attention to the style, visual appearance, and communication skills demonstrated by your resume through the entire resume writing process.

2. Remember to ask yourself three questions when deciding what information to include on your resume:

    A. Is the information absolutely necessary?
    B. Does the information provide a positive representation of you?
    C. Is the information true (factual)?

3. Initially, resumes are more likely to be scanned rather than read closely. Make sure your resume highlights the important facts without a thorough reading.

4. Write at least two rough drafts of your resume and get the objective opinions of others in each phase before going to your final draft.

5. If you are applying for a job in more than one field, prepare a separate resume for each field.

Questions for Review

1. The primary function of the resume is to list your experience and credentials. What else can preparing a resume do for you?

2. What are the three major types of resume formats? Which of the formats is best for you?

3. What are the basic elements of a resume?

4. You can choose from three different methods to describe the various stages of your career. What are they?

5. Should you include references as part of your resume?

6. Is it appropriate for you to have more than one resume?

7. What are the basics to remember when preparing a resume?

Chapter Seven:
Planning for Success

You will be whatever you resolve to be. Determine to be something in the world and you will be something. "I cannot" never accomplished anything. "I will" has wrought wonders.

Joel Hawes

The Importance of Planning

Many career decisions are based upon emotion rather than rational thought. When you decide to make a career change you are more likely to be successful if your decision involves informed and effective planning. A career change is like a marketing project. Planning, research, promotion, and persistence are all required to achieve success. Simply putting together a resume and responding to newspaper ads is not a responsible approach to a career change—a strategy must be developed.

After assessing your skills and exploring the market you will need to identify the steps that will be required for you to reach your goal. It may be easier to do this if you first identify some of the difficulties people face in making a career change.

One of the primary challenges people face is overcoming **procrastination**. This is particularly true for people who are driven by emotion in their desire for a career change, because the amount of energy that is spent on a job search is affected by the amount of emotion that is fueling it. For instance, a disagreement with a supervisor might make someone feel like changing jobs right away. However, this type of motivation does not usually last very long; people lose interest in a career change as their emotion fades. When the emotion fades, so does the energy required to carry out a successful career change. People in this situation generally put off making the change until emotion again pushes them to take action.

Ask yourself why you want to change your job or your career. Is it based on an emotional decision, or a rational one? If it is a rational decision, realize that nothing is going to change until you take action. If your decision is an emotional one, realize that your commitment to career change will vary as much as your emotions do.

Another difficulty you may encounter is the **illusion** of effort. It is not uncommon for people to focus a great deal of attention on writing beautiful resumes. They often invest a lot of time in the resume and show it to others for advice. This makes them feel like they have accomplished something. However, the resume is only a small part in the entire process. It is very important, but it is not the only means of locating career opportunities. Resumes are important tools; but they are only tools—nothing more. Therefore, don't expect too much of your resume. It is easy to fool yourself into thinking you are using your energy productively when, in fact, you are merely wasting it.

Responding to advertisements for positions you are not qualified for is another illusion of effort. People sometimes respond to ads even if they are not qualified for the position, hoping they will get an interview anyway. This is usually a waste of time—time that would be better spent working on something more productive.

Developing a Strategic Plan

People who use little or no strategy in making a career change tend to follow a standard pattern. Typically, their approach includes creating a resume, responding to ads, interviewing, and accepting or refusing an offer. This approach often results in either no change, or merely a simple change of jobs rather than an optimal career move.

A self-directed approach increases your awareness of the opportunities that are available to you and promotes long-term career satisfaction. This approach is based upon a comprehensive view of yourself regarding career opportunity. Figure 7-1 illustrates the steps in the process.

As demonstrated in Figure 7-1, there are a number of important steps that should be taken before beginning to write your resume. In addition to following these steps, it is helpful to write out what you intend to do during each phase as well as the expected completion dates.

To use a self-directed approach, it is important that you understand the different elements in the process. They include a **career goal**, **objectives**, **milestones**, and **activities**.

- Your career goal is what you want and expect to achieve (i.e., own business, vice president of marketing with major firm, become osteopathic physician, increase promotion potential with current employer, etc.).

- Your objectives are the short-term goals that must be achieved in order to reach your career goal (i.e., leave current job, develop new career focus, identify and obtain improved opportunity, become well respected in new position, etc.).

- Milestones are the steps that must be completed within specific time frames in order to reach your goal (i.e., complete market exploration by November 1, develop list of advisors by November 5, etc.).

- Activities are the specific tasks that must be completed to fulfill your milestone deadlines (i.e., library research, contact list calls, first draft of resume, etc.).

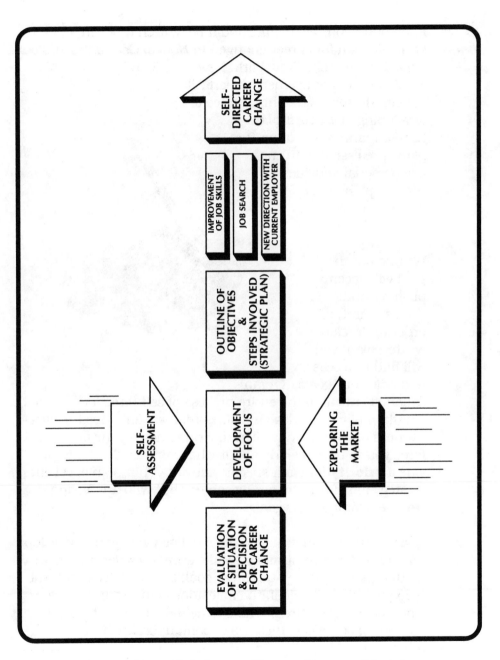

Figure 7–1: Mid-Career Change Process Model

Each of the four elements should be written down in a strategic plan for career change. In *How to Get Control of Your Time and Your Life* (New York: New American Library, 1974, c1973), time-management expert Allan Lakein, discusses the importance of developing a **written plan**. Lakein maintains that written plans are essential to control personal activities. Written plans force you to become organized.

Writing out the plan will accomplish a number of things. First, in order to develop a written plan, you will find it necessary to define your goals. Organization is critical to the entire process of self-direction. Second, a written plan provides guidelines that will enhance the effectiveness of your actions. Third, writing down your plan will force you to think clearly about what must be done and provide a **priority** for each specific activity. This is an excellent strategy for those who are discontent but who are having trouble defining their goals.

Use whatever format makes the most sense to you to develop an outline for your strategy. Make sure, however, that your written plan defines your career goal, the objectives that will help you attain the goal, the milestones, and your activities. Don't worry if you are not able to define all the activities in your plan; some activities will depend upon the outcome of other activities.

Case Study—A Strategic Plan

Here is an example of how a written strategic plan for career change might look.

Mary was employed as a director of purchasing at a small manufacturer of materials used in electronic components. The business is privately owned and its operations are conducted at three plants within a 15 mile radius of each other. The firm employs approximately 250 people.

Mary has served as director of purchasing for three years, having worked her way up from a buyer position over an 11 year span. She previously worked as a buyer for an automotive supplier. Mary has a bachelor's degree in business. She has two children and is 38 years old.

Recently, Mary concluded that she has no opportunity for continued career growth with her current employer. The company has little to offer in terms of upward mobility. Since Mary is not a member of the family that owns the business, she believes her opportunities for further advancement are severely limited.

Mary is ambitious. She wants to increase her income, and even more important, she wants the chance to increase her responsibility and take on new challenges. As a result, she has decided to search for new opportunities elsewhere. She began her strategic plan with a goal which provides focus for her direction. Her plan also included supporting objectives which help describe the type of opportunity she seeks. She wrote them as follows:

I. GOAL

Move from current position as director of purchasing of privately held small business to facilities or materials purchasing manager of larger firm in which I will have opportunity for increasing advancement.

II. OBJECTIVES

A. Obtain work that is more professionally fulfilling (re: challenge, creativity, and long-term growth potential).

B. Increase income potential.

C. Achieve career change without need to relocate family unless relocation trade-offs meet or exceed current situational advantages.

So far, this example expresses Mary's desire to pursue an opportunity with greater long-term potential. Her objectives also include the fact that she would like to make this change without uprooting her family unless the benefits of such a move outweigh the change in location.

Now let's look at some of her milestones and related activities. (Notice that they follow the steps shown in Figure 7–1.) Since she has already made up her mind to search for new opportunity, her first milestone has already been reached. Also notice that one of her activities is a mental process. She must accept the fact that she has limited opportunity for growth with her present employer.

III. MILESTONES

A. Decision for career change made on January 1. Activities included:

1. Formal discussion with current supervisor regarding future advancement.

2. Awareness of limited potential with current employer.

3. Find ways to improve my career growth potential.

B. Self-Assessment (To be completed by January 21.) Activities include:

1. Develop list of current marketable skills.

2. Participate in assessment of interview skills (i.e., attend interview workshop offered through local college).

3. Visit with career counselor.

C. Exploring the market (To be completed by February 12.) Activities include:

1. Visit public library to research appropriate business directories in order to target local firms that may need people with my background.

2. Identify professional associations that can provide information regarding likely employers.

3. Develop a list of business contacts who may provide advice on how and where to identify existing or potential openings for which I may apply.

4. Identify publications which are likely sources of information on business growth and employment opportunities for which I am qualified.

D. Development of Specific Focus (To be completed by March 1.) Activities include:

1. Make decision on restricting search to facilities and materials purchasing or consider other operations management positions.

2. Identify most likely industries which will offer best career and income potential.

3. Establish perspective on my willingness to relocate and the considerations that will be included in a relocation decision.

E. Analyze and Refine Objectives and Steps in Process (To be completed by March 10.) Activities include:

1. Continue to write this plan after gathering information by performing all the activities outlined in milestones A through D.

As demonstrated in this example, the process involves a sequence of events. Certain steps cannot be completed without first fulfilling others. As a result, Mary must assess her skills and explore the market before she can identify the specific vehicles and network contacts that will help lead her to new opportunities. In addition, decisions to be made along the way (including time deadlines) are not possible without first performing the required research. Milestone E shows this. Before she can continue with her plan, Mary must gather and analyze the information she has obtained up to that point.

If Mary performs all of the steps included in her plan up to March 10th, she will be well prepared to begin an employment search. She will have considered her personal and family needs, assessed her marketable skills and researched the market. Most important, Mary will have established the direction of her career change based upon well informed and rational considerations.

Some people may not be comfortable with a written plan that is as structured as the one Mary used. This is fine. What is important about the strategic approach is not how detailed or formal your actual outline is, but that you take the time to become informed and think carefully about how you will reach your goal. Do your homework and establish a plan. Do not base a career change on pure emotional response. You may end up in an uncomfortable situation.

After Mary completes all activities required by her March 10th deadline, she will be ready to move to the second phase in her career change. If she is still interested in leaving her current employer, she will define the steps she must take to initiate a formal job hunt. This is identified as *job search* in Figure 7-1.

It is important to note that Figure 7-1 names two other options above and below the job search box. They are *improve job skills* and *new direction with current employer*. These options refer to the fact that sometimes self-assessment and market exploration indicate that it may be better to work toward improving career opportunity with your current employer than looking outside. Improved career opportunity may require some adjustment or effort on your part that will result in your being placed elsewhere in the organization. The phrase *self-directed career change* in Figure 7-1 emphasizes the fact that the final result depends upon your deliberate and planned effort rather than on luck or the decisions of others.

In the job search phase of her career change, Mary again lists milestones and related activities. These may include completion dates for development of her resume; contacting the alumni placement office of her university alma mater; contacting people who may be able to identify specific job openings; and responding to openings listed in newspapers and professional journals.

Organizational Tools

The most important tool in making a mid-career change is a well-developed strategic plan. In addition, there are a number of related techniques that should be considered. You should use at least three support tools such as contact lists (or a diary), a filing system, and a binder.

A filing system that organizes all of the research and support information you gather can be very useful. Information gained from market exploration, self-assessment, and resume development should be included in this system, as well as your strategic plan, correspondence, source and network contacts, resumes, etc.

Some people like to store such information on their personal
computer. A computer can be very helpful; but unless you
have a portable one, you will have to spend extra time
updating your computer files using your notes.

Contact lists are records of people you have contacted as
advisors, resources, or network contacts. It is important to
keep the names, telephone numbers, dates contacted, and
outcome of the discussions well documented. See Figure 7-2.
These contacts are most likely going to be the heart of your
search process. You will need to refer back to them frequently
during your job search. Some people like to record such
contacts in a
diary format,
including the
dates and
action result-
ing from such
contacts. A
diary format
is a good
method. It
allows you
to keep a
complete
record of all
contacts made,
their recommendations, follow-up action you take, and dates
of such action. In addition, all such information must allow
quick and easy reference.

A binder is useful if you are responding to various advertisements and open postings. You should keep copies of all ads
to which you respond, the dates of the ad, and your response.
If you get a reply, you will want to be able to make quick
reference to any information you have about the opening.
Often, the ad may be the only source of information you have.

DATE	CONTACT/PHONE	RESULT
3/18/93	Tom Nelson 409-555-3046	Discussed possible strategy for job change. He suggested calling Mary Sween at 409-555-1458.
3/18/93	Mary Sween 409-555-1458	Out until 3/24/93. Call her back then.
3/18/93	George Brown 409-555-0046	He suggested contacting Sam Trent of his company (Trent is Human Resource Manager.)
3/18/93	Sam Trent 409-555-0046	Trent wants copy of resume. Agreed to provide me with some word by 4-1.
3/18/93	Cathy Stewart 409-555-1770	Stewart had little time to talk. Suggested I send resume and call back 3-25.
3/20/93	Troy Donald 513-555-8240	Discussed use of Pro-Search data network. Suggested entering credentials.
3/20/93	Bill Townsend 409-555-8643	Out till 3/22. Call back then.
3/20/93	Terry Smith 409-555-3342	Didn't seem interested in talking with me. Doubt if he can be of any help.

Figure 7–2: Contact List

Finally, remember that you will never reach your goal without first defining one. The process of defining the goal must be based upon rational considerations resulting from thorough research. The goal should be expressed in a deliberate written plan. The plan is not set in concrete at the beginning but remains flexible to accommodate new information as you acquire it. Don't become so over-organized that keeping records and information keeps you from pursuing your goal. Your organization plan should help you achieve a goal, it is not the goal itself.

Strategic Planning Tips

1. Plan to use a rational and systematic process to ensure successful career change.

2. Do not allow procrastination to deter your progress.

3. Spend your time on truly productive activities. Avoid creating an illusion of productivity.

4. Make adequate use of planners, filing systems, lists of contacts, calendars, etc.

5. Decide how you will enlist others to help you in this project.

6. Write out your complete strategic plan including at least the basic objectives and milestones as best you can before beginning.

7. Keep all your records up to date.

Questions for Review

1. Name four of the most common difficulties people may face in making a career change.

2. What steps should be taken before beginning to write your resume?

3. Describe the strategic approach and its benefits.

4. What organizational tools are helpful?

5. What are the benefits of developing and using a written plan?

Chapter Eight:

Marketing Your Talents

Make the most of yourself for that is all there is to you.

Ralph Waldo Emerson

The Importance of Marketing Yourself

Searching for new career opportunities can be one of the most significant challenges of your life. There are many avenues to follow and you may want to explore one or many of them to reach your objective. We will examine some of those options in this chapter. It is important to realize that your success in a job search is not determined solely on your past achievements or credentials, but also by how you present that information to prospective employers. Although at first it appears quite intimidating, a job search can be one of the most positive learning experiences of your life. Searching for new employment is an excellent lesson in marketing. The product is you, and the market is as broad as you make it.

The most important aspect of this marketing effort is the fact that ultimate success is based upon convincing someone to offer you an opportunity. However, no one is going to give you an opportunity unless you can provide him or her with a confident feeling about you. Therefore, people who are skilled in human relations have the greatest chance for success.

If you have an accurate view of your interpersonal skills, have explored the market; possess a well-conceived strategic plan; and have a well-written resume, your efforts during the job search stand a much higher chance for success. However, the manner in which you perform these steps will greatly affect the number of opportunities that will be offered to you.

There are many ways to locate new employment opportunities. This chapter addresses seven broad categories and describes techniques for making the most of them. They include:

- Networking contacts.
- Direct application to targeted organizations.
- Response to advertisements.

- Use of open posting systems.

- Contacting recruiters.

- Employment agencies.

- Outplacement assistance.

Networking Contacts

Networking is one of the most effective means of finding employment. The majority of positions, other than entry level, are filled by interpersonal contacts and referrals. Networking includes the contacts you made when you explored the market and builds upon them. The term **networking** refers to the direct contacts you make (usually by telephone) in order to identify potential employment through informal discussions. Networking applies a referral approach; you ask almost every person you talk with if they can refer you to someone else to contact.

To network successfully, you must identify highly visible and respected people in your industry or field. Their advice and perspective on how you might identify improved career opportunities will be extremely valuable. Let them know that you are open to opportunities and send them a copy of your resume if you feel it is appropriate.

The networking strategy is based upon the development of an information network that leads to referral sources. One of the primary differences between this approach and simply sending resumes to advertisements is that this approach does not lead to a specific end. It does not lead to a *yes* or *no* concerning a particular job opportunity; instead, it develops additional contacts that lead to other information sources. Employment opportunities will be revealed in the process. There are three phases in this approach; developing a source list, making contacts, and following up your leads.

The Source List

The source list includes the names of individuals who may be aware of potential positions. They are not necessarily the people who make hiring decisions. The source list is developed from two primary groups. The first group is made up of individuals you know personally. The second group consists of people you have never met but who are well known and who know many others in the field that interests you.

Contacting people you have never met is called **cold calling**. It is not easy to make cold calls, but they are essential to a well-balanced source list. If you network the first group effectively, the people you call should refer you to the people who will make up the second group. Hopefully, you will develop most of the names on your cold call list through referrals from people you do know. However, you may have to target some key people for cold calls without the benefit of referral or introduction from others.

Developing your source list is crucial to the success of your plan for career change. To develop the source list of personal contacts, you may follow this suggested sequence. To begin, identify the types of positions for which you want to be considered. Your exploration of the market should help you make this decision. This does not necessarily mean that all of the positions have to be exactly the same type. However, the positions should fall into two or three categories (by occupation and industry) so that source contacts may be developed in those areas.

As you begin to develop your source contact list (first group), work in reverse chronological order. Start with your most recent contacts and work backward to the people you knew in college and high school. Think of the individuals you have worked with, met at conventions, or made acquaintances with who may be knowledgeable in your area of interest. Focus on individuals who have high visibility in organizations or industries. These individuals may know about potential vacancies or at least know someone else who may be familiar with potential vacancies.

The source list of cold contacts (second group) is developed by following up on referrals from people you know, contacting organizations which interest you, reviewing appropriate directories, attending association meetings, etc.

Source Calls

The contacts you make using your source list will help you set your objectives. Your source list should not be used simply as a source for general information. Do not simply telephone these people and tell them you are looking for a job and ask them to alert you if they become aware of any openings. A successful approach requires that you telephone the contact and determine his or her willingness to speak with you. If it is not a good time to speak with you, tell him or her that you will call back and ask when you should. If you have called at an appropriate time, tell the individual you are making some career decisions and you would appreciate his or her advice. Explain that one of the options you are considering is to make a transition into either: (a) the type of organization for which the contact works, or (b) the type of industry or occupation in which the contact is employed. Do not mention that you are looking for a job. Tell your contact that you would like to ask a couple of questions, and his or her advice would be much appreciated. The first question is, "How can I best prepare myself for an opportunity in this type of career?" You should also ask, "What would you do to identify opportunities in this type of setting or organization?"

The second line of questioning is even more important. It is, "Do you know of anyone who might be helpful in advising me of where potential opportunities may exist?" This question is really the essence of the conversation. If the individual you are calling says, "No, I don't have any advice," or "I don't know of any contacts," you might respond, "Okay, but would you mind giving it some thought?" Chances are, your contact is going to agree to this. Wind up your phone call by asking, "May I call you back in a week or two to find out if you have thought of any contact people?" This sets an objective for the contact. By setting a specific time for a return call, you increase the probability that your contact  will have information later. The more calls you make, the more referrals to other people you will receive. As you build a base of advisors you will gain more and more valuable information and come closer to identifying job leads. This is what networking is all about.

If you simply call someone and ask, "Do you know of a job?" the person may simply say "No, I don't." This is a dead-end contact. However, when you make contact and say, "Do you have advice?" or "Do you know of other resource people?" you will be more likely to at least receive another name, if not information or advice which might lead you toward a job opportunity. This type of questioning generally leads to a response because you are merely asking for information. By asking these questions, you also leave open the possibility that your contact may actually refer you to an opening.

The networking procedure requires a systematic approach. You should set up a binder in which you record all contacts, the name and phone number, date called, advice or names of other referred contacts, or when you will call them back. Be sure to send your contacts a note thanking them for their time and help. You also can send them a copy of your resume if you feel it is appropriate.

Follow Up

Make regular calls and follow up all leads. An approach which can help is to set a performance standard. For example, make four or five calls a day for five days out of the week. This way you can accomplish 20 to 25 primary source calls in a week's time. In two weeks you can do anywhere from 40 to 50 calls. Some of those calls are probably going to generate referred contacts or good advice. It is important to make that referred contact the same day while it is fresh in your mind and you know how to best approach the contact.

It is also important to ask everyone who refers you to someone else, "Do you mind if I mention your name so the new contact will know who referred me?" More than likely, the source contact is not going to mind if you mention his or her name. This ready-made reference gives you more credibility when you make the call. It is also best for you to make referral calls yourself, rather than leave it up to the person referring you. This increases the likelihood of immediate action and does not burden your original contact.

One of the biggest obstacles to overcome in the process of networking is rejection or dead-end leads. This is unavoid-able, but you must remain optimistic. Remember, it only takes one contact of the right kind to get connected—so keep at it and don't take rejection personally. Usually, the rejection is not a rejection of you personally. Instead, rejections usually mean that you are simply not the person who is best suited for that particular position.

This entire networking approach is designed to lead you to people in positions of visibility or influence. In fact, it is some-thing you should do even when you are not planning to leave your job. It is always a good idea to keep in touch with people in your field and other fields that interest you. You never know when you may need their help! By maintaining contact with these people, you will be notified when positions for which you are qualified become available. In addition, it is important for you to set a goal for how many calls you will make per week. This is particularly true with making cold calls. For example, a goal of 20 cold calls a week is plenty if you are actively looking for a career change. Setting that particular goal makes it easier to get through the list. If you do not set a goal, it will be easy to give up after four to five calls of being put off or not being able to reach your party. Do not get discouraged! Chances are, positive results will begin to occur before you have made all 20 calls. However, regard-less of the results you receive, make all the calls you planned. Remember, the more calls you make, the better informed and effective you will become. This process not only educates you about where opportunities may exist, but also increases the likelihood of being visible to recruiters or people who need to hire someone like you. Remember—networking is a way of *reaching* your goal, it is not *the* goal.

Applying for a Job—Direct Application

Direct application means that you are applying directly to a company or organization for a position. To do this, you must either target the organization as a place you would like to work, or you must have knowledge of a specific need for someone with your qualifications.

Applying for a Specific Opening

If you are applying directly for a specific position, you have at least two options. First, you may apply through the established procedure. This usually includes submitting a cover letter and a resume to the employment office and completing an application. In this case, your chances of getting an interview will be affected by three considerations. These considerations include: the strength of your qualifications; the power of your cover letter and resume; and your compensation range. You have a lot of control over all but the first of these variables.

The Cover Letter

As mentioned before, the appearance of your resume does not change your qualifications, but the way your qualifications are packaged can enhance the perception of your ability. This applies to your cover letter too. The cover letter provides potential employers with their first impression of you. If your cover letter fails to make a good impression, they may not even look at your resume. Therefore, you should draft your cover letter with great care. The cover letter should achieve four specific objectives:

1.   It should be more specific in stating your case than a resume.

2.   It should state the position for which you are applying.

3.   It should establish the **context** of your **credentials**.

4.   It should make a positive enough impression to build the reader's interest in you.

A cover letter is different than a resume in that you have the opportunity to tailor it to a specific situation. It takes the place of an objective statement on the resume and, in fact, is one of the reasons that putting an objective on the resume is optional. If your resume is accompanied by a cover letter, it really does not need an objective.

A cover letter written in respect to a specific opening normally includes three sections. The first section references the position for which you are applying. This can be done in a brief paragraph which includes any additional information which should be mentioned—such as referral by a second party. The second section refers to your credentials. Highlight your strongest qualifications which most relate to the position for which you are applying. The second section may also include a statement as to why this particular position is so interesting to you. The third section finishes with a suggested course of action, (i.e., I will contact you within 10 days, etc.). See Example 8-1.

1861 Lincoln
Englewood, CO 34715

Barbara Simms
Director of Engineering
Mipstad Corporation
1234 Santa Fe
San Francisco, CA 61634

Dear Ms. Simms:

Mr. William Donaldson of the Mipstad Corporation Research and Development
Department recommended I send you a copy of my resume. I would like to be
considered for the opening you have as Supervisor of New Product Engineering.

As you can tell on my resume, my background has prepared me for this position.
With six years in new product engineering for a firm that produces satellite electronic
components, I also have over three years of supervisory experience. Included in my
supervisory experience is managing a staff of seven product development specialists.

I also have a master's degree in Electrical Engineering with emphasis on artificial
intelligence systems from XYZ University.

I would appreciate your contacting me at your earliest convenience to discuss the
opening further. You may reach me at (303) 555-9214 during the evening and on
weekends.

 Thank you for your consideration.

Sincerely,

Tom Larkin

Tom Larkin

Enclosure

Example 8-1: Cover Letter

Another variable you can control is your compensation range. If you can, find out the compensation range of the position before you apply. This will prepare you in case your salary expectations are requested on the application. Being positioned in the low to middle of the compensation range is usually best, providing you will be satisfied at this level.

Your second option in applying to a specific position is to make direct contact with the decision maker in the process. The idea behind this approach is to gain the attention of the decision maker. When this is done properly, you will stand out from the rest of the applicants in a favorable way. This does not mean that you bypass the established application procedure. It is generally best to follow it, and supplement it with the direct contact approach. When using the direct contact approach, you will be attempting to have a conversation, either in-person or by telephone, with the decision maker prior to the planned interview. Generally speaking, this can be quite difficult to accomplish. Some approaches to consider include:

1. An introduction or referral by someone inside the organization. This can help you learn whether or not the position is something for which you should apply.

2. A direct **cold call** to the decision maker by you.

3. A third party presenting your credentials to the decision maker (without you being present) to promote your chances for an interview.

Items one and three are preferable if they can be arranged. If they cannot, item two, which requires courage, tact, and diplomacy may be your only option. Unfortunately, it also carries a low chance of success. However, if it can be managed, it can be worth all of the potential frustrations which may accompany a cold call.

I Want to See Them, But Do They Want to See Me?

What if a potential employer doesn't want to see you? This is a problem for many mid-career change seekers. The best approach is to assume that employers will want to see you. More employers will see you than you may think if you make the effort to see them. Do not make generalizations about employers. The secret is to find those that will talk to you and proceed from there.

The best way to find employers who will speak to you is to do your homework—identify employers who have a need for someone like you. Take a positive approach. Assume that you can help them and they can help you. It's a two-way street. Don't assume that the employer holds all the cards and that you are subject to their whims. Your attitude will have an impact on the people you see and on how confident you feel in the interview process.

Targeted Organizations/Non-Specific Opening

When you apply for a non-specific opening, you apply to an organization without knowing of a particular opening for which you are well suited. In this case, you suspect the organization now needs, or may soon need, someone with your background. While the general procedures for contact are similar to those for a specific opening, there are some distinct differences.

Since there is no specific position for which to apply, you must focus heavily upon finding a contact person within the organization. Your preliminary research must be thorough enough to yield the name or names of people who will be most likely to present you with a job opportunity. Try to speak to this person either face-to-face, or by telephone. Don't limit your contact with this person to written correspondence unless it is absolutely necessary. You may use the same contact techniques that you would for an application to a specific opening, but remember—the focus is now different. Rather than trying to obtain information about a particular opening, you are attempting to get information about the *potential* for an opening for which you are qualified. The object of this type of contact is to get advice about the potential for opportunity in that organization. You will also be trying to obtain referrals to other key people within the organization.

Make sure that you follow up your initial contacts with a phone call or letter. This is important for specific openings, but even more so for non-specific openings. If someone needs to fill a specific opening and is interested in you, he or she will contact you. However, when you are trying to find out about the potential of a position, *you* are the one with the higher level of interest. The people you contact may not remember you when a position becomes available unless you remind them of your interest. Therefore, more emphasis must be placed upon staying in touch in order to respond to an opportunity as soon as it appears.

Responding to Advertisements

Responding to advertisements can be worthwhile as long as you have the qualifications the position requires. Respond only to advertisements for which you are qualified. It is usually a mistake to *shotgun* responses to a lot of advertisements for which you are only remotely qualified; this is more likely to waste your time than yield results. However, if you see an advertisement which interests you, and you have the necessary qualifications, respond! Once again, a strong resume and a well-written cover letter are essential.

When responding to an advertisement, the cover letter should reflect much the same format as a direct contact cover letter. However, there are at least two differences. One difference is in the introductory paragraph. It is here that you will refer to the specific advertisement to which you are responding. See Example 8-2. The second difference is a statement of compensation expectations. Many advertisements will ask you to state your salary requirements or your salary history. In this case you should provide rounded figures (i.e., earning low 50s or seeking mid-50s, etc.).

It is not always necessary to respond immediately to advertisements. Allow yourself time to think carefully about the qualifications for which they are looking. Write a strong cover letter to accompany your resume. Sometimes, it is best to delay sending your resume for a while to ensure that it is likely to be received by itself or with just a few others. This way, your resume is more likely to get the attention it deserves. Keep a record of all advertisements to which you respond. This will help you be alert to any response you may receive. You should sound as if you expect a response when you speak to potential employers on the phone. You also should keep a record of all the people to whom you speak regarding responses, interview dates, etc.

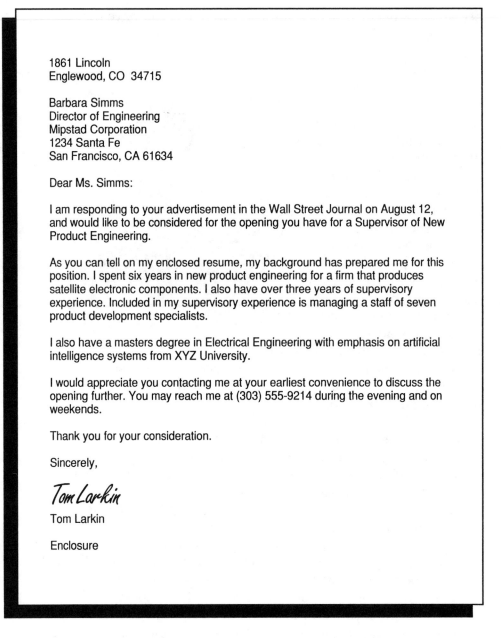

1861 Lincoln
Englewood, CO 34715

Barbara Simms
Director of Engineering
Mipstad Corporation
1234 Santa Fe
San Francisco, CA 61634

Dear Ms. Simms:

I am responding to your advertisement in the Wall Street Journal on August 12, and would like to be considered for the opening you have for a Supervisor of New Product Engineering.

As you can tell on my enclosed resume, my background has prepared me for this position. I spent six years in new product engineering for a firm that produces satellite electronic components. I also have over three years of supervisory experience. Included in my supervisory experience is managing a staff of seven product development specialists.

I also have a masters degree in Electrical Engineering with emphasis on artificial intelligence systems from XYZ University.

I would appreciate you contacting me at your earliest convenience to discuss the opening further. You may reach me at (303) 555-9214 during the evening and on weekends.

Thank you for your consideration.

Sincerely,

Tom Larkin

Tom Larkin

Enclosure

Example 8-2: Cover Letter to Advertisement

Normally, you will have at least three sources of advertisements. The most common sources are local newspapers. While they list large numbers of openings, there are several drawbacks that reduce their potential for most job seekers. One drawback is the large number of responses to the better positions. Your resume can get lost in the shuffle. This is one of the reasons you should wait a few days before sending your resume. Most people send theirs immediately. If you wait to send yours, it will be more likely to get noticed. Another drawback is that newspaper advertisements typically don't tell you much about the opening. This makes it difficult to know whether the position is worth responding to and what to emphasize in your cover letter.

A second source of advertisements are the regional and national publications. Many of the Fortune 500 companies routinely advertise through these publications. While these offer many excellent opportunities, the competition is often much greater. It is not unusual for a well-written *Wall Street Journal* advertisement to draw 500 to 1,000 responses in a week's time.

In addition to newspapers, consider trade journals, business and professional publications, and magazines. In these cases, response time is an even less critical factor. The advertisers often expect to have to wait awhile for the proper exposure to their readers. Do not wait *too* long though; you never know how quickly they might need to fill the position.

Job Posting Systems

Federal government recruiting departments, state security systems, college and university placement offices, state recruiting departments, and professional association job clearinghouses are all examples of formalized job posting systems. These systems may be excellent sources of employment for you to consider. In some cases, you may have to meet certain requirements before entering the system.

For example, you may have to be a member of a particular profes- sional association to gain access to their clearinghouse, or you may have to be a graduate of a specific university to use their placement office.

Most people overlook such sources of opportunity. As a result, the competition for openings is not as great as it is in response to advertisements or direct contact to personnel offices. However, be prepared. These routes often involve a lengthy selection process.

Recruiters

Outside the sphere of employment agencies and corporate personnel departments lies a very large and significant indus- try of specialists. These professionals may be called executive search consultants, speciality recruiters, or any of a number of other titles. They differ from employment agencies in that they do not promote walk-ins or large banks of people seeking employment. In addition, many of these recruiters have retainer arrangements with their clients (the employer) and are paid increments as they perform their services rather than a pure commission upon placement.

These firms usually fill positions at the management and executive levels. They often work for a specific client, and find their candidates through network contacts and specific advertising. This is not always a good source of opportunity for everyone, but it can be helpful for some. For example, skill areas that are in high demand (such as the medical field) often have recruiting firms that specialize in such areas. These recruiters welcome contact from people with strong credentials in these areas.

Find out if there are recruiting firms that specialize in such areas. Such firms advertise in professional journals or can be identified through their membership in professional associations. You will find additional information on the recruiting industry in Appendix B.

There are three different types of recruiters. Understanding how they differ will help you determine which, if any of them, may be of help to you.

Retainer recruiters are paid a pre-established sum of money for their recruiting work. They usually receive the payment in three increments. The first increment is received when they begin the assignment, the second increment is billed at a set time during the assignment, and the third increment is due after successful completion of the recruitment effort. Because they get paid for their effort regardless of the outcome, they can afford to screen candidates very carefully before presenting them to the client company. As a result, you need to be well prepared to discuss your specific skills and abilities when communicating with retainer recruiters. You will find examples of retainer recruiters listed in Appendix C.

Contingency recruiters are paid an established fee or percentage only when one of their candidates is hired, regardless of the number of candidates that have been referred. As a result, they have more incentive to place greater emphasis on attracting as many candidates as possible and promoting their merits to the person who makes the hiring decision. You can find this type of recruiter through their advertisements in newspapers and business publications. Contingency recruiters differ from personnel agencies only when the recruiter's service is based upon active candidate development by means other than taking walk-ins. Additional information on agency recruiters is included in Appendix G.

Corporate recruiters are employees of the hiring company. They are paid a normal annual salary on an ongoing basis regardless of how many people they recruit. An example of a corporate recruiter is a college recruiter. Often, they are not under as much pressure as contingency recruiters to sell you on the opportunity. You often find these recruiters through their advertisements in newspapers, journals, and by contacting the corporate employment office of the firm in which you are interested.

Recruiters are paid for performing a difficult task—locating and attracting well-qualified candidates. Well-qualified candidates do not just happen to show up at recruiters' door steps. Finding them is often quite difficult. Recruiters have to know how to find them. They use the **mainstream**. The mainstream is the network of people in particular industries, fields or professions who are aware of strong professionals who may be open to job opportunities. Recruiters access this source by staying in touch with key people in professions and industries where candidates with the type of background they seek are likely to be found. When you network, you are doing the same thing that they do.

Recruiters must go to the mainstream to develop leads for candidates. They usually do this by telephone or through personal contacts to well-respected people in the industry. From this, you should be able to see the importance of not relying just on filling out applications or responding to newspaper ads. You are going to have to appear in the mainstream as well; you must let it be known to key and well-connected professionals that you are looking for a change in employment. Making these contacts is part of networking. Do this by telephone or in person. Don't rely on written correspondence for this important step.

In making direct contact with recruiters, remember that many others may be trying to do the same; therefore, it may be difficult. Try to identify those recruiters who are most likely to handle your career specialty. If possible, have someone who knows such a recruiter **sponsor** you. Also, telephoning first thing in the morning and following up later if they are out gives you a little better chance of making contact.

Trade Secrets of Recruiters

Professional recruiters are relatively quiet about their methods. These recruiters are usually highly trained and well paid for what they do. See Appendix D. They have to be skilled to survive in their world because of the extreme competition and "hard ball" business practices that are prevalent in their industry.

An understanding of the key practices recruiters use to "stay alive" and prevail in their business may be helpful to you as you encounter such recruiters.

1.   A recruiter's top priority for success is to please his or her clients. The candidate's interests are of less importance. However, the recruiter will try to refer well-qualified candidates (with excellent interpersonal and interviewing skills) who will be well matched to the opening and who will be likely to stay in the position for a long time. This, in turn, works in the candidate's favor by increasing the likelihood of gaining a position for which he or she is well suited.

2.   Recruiters know how to *sell* a position and present it in an attractive light. If the candidate responds well to this, the recruiter is more likely to present that candidate to the client because high interest and enthusiasm increase the odds of successful placement.

3.   The most effective recruiters are very well connected. They know many key people in the industries they recruit in and use these respected individuals to refer well-qualified candidates. If one of these key contacts knows you, and is aware of your interest in searching for a new opportunity, he or she may be able to refer you to a recruiter.

4.   Recruiters use the telephone as their primary screening device in separating the best candidates from the rest of the pack. Consider any such call an interview, and be alert to cues and critical discussion points including the essence of your current job or career status, your desired compensation range, and the overall strength of your credentials. Also, remember that how alert and intelligent you sound on the telephone is going to have a significant effect upon the recruiter.

5. The in-person interview will often be used by the recruiter to focus more upon your interpersonal skills and suitability for their client's work setting than your technical qualifications. Technical qualifications will also be assessed carefully, but recruiters will be looking for much more.

6. Effective recruiters know how to obtain real facts about your background from references. They have the ability to see through the generalizations that references may offer and unearth details and critical incidents, as well as names of other supervisors or references you did not offer! As a result, you should always be completely honest and candid regarding your references. Furthermore, you should advise your references of the positions for which the recruiter is screening you.

7. Lastly, the best recruiters know their reputation and long-term success is contingent upon the reputation and long-term success of the candidates they place with their clients. Your past record and your conduct must indicate such potential every step of the way when dealing with recruiters.

Employment Agencies

Employment agencies fall into two general categories. The most common category includes those who charge a fee to companies for referring applicants to them. This kind of employment agency usually does not collect a fee unless one of the applicants they refer gets hired. This hiring fee is usually a percentage of the first year's salary. It will cost you nothing to work with an employment agency of this type. The other type of employment agency charges *you* a fee if they are instrumental in locating a position for you. Many people are reluctant to use these firms because of this.

Many fine employment agencies provide excellent services to their clients and opportunities for candidates. However, some agencies do not meet such standards. Research employment agencies carefully before contacting them. Do this by talking to others who have first-hand knowledge of them. If you are unable to find anyone with this information on your own, ask the agency for several references. If you can speak with some of the people the agency has successfully placed, you can be reasonably sure of getting some reliable feedback regarding the agency's success rate.

Some agency personnel call themselves executive recruiters or professional recruiters. This is true if they develop candidates through active means other than advertising or offering a walk-in office setup. However, their basic service usually includes straight matching or referral of candidates on file against listed positions on file. Agencies usually do less screening and background checking than recruiters. Agencies are paid a commission or percentage of the new hire's first year's compensation. However, they only collect their fee when they refer someone who is hired and shows up for work. This fee may be based upon a graduated scale that is keyed to the first year's total compensation. Basically, they are actually contingency recruiters.

Outplacement Services

Outplacement counselors are usually not direct sources of job opportunities. They generally charge a fee for advice regarding new career paths, job search skills, resume and interviewing techniques, skills assessment, identification of aptitudes and interests, and other counseling services. These firms typically do not steer you toward specific job openings, but teach you skills designed to enhance your ability to identify new opportunities, interview, and negotiate employment opportunities. However, some outplacement firms have cooperative agreements with professional recruiters or job network systems and may occasionally steer job seekers to new opportunities. These instances are rather rare though. Be aware that some outplacement firms have the majority of their business coming from contract work with organizations and may not offer services to individuals. These firms focus their services on assisting displaced professionals who have lost their jobs, and the employer usually pays the fees. Outplacement counselor's fees can be as much as 15% of your most recent year's salary. Since they primarily teach techniques to supplement your own methods, you may pay them a considerable fee and receive little for it if your job search expertise is already high. Research these firms carefully before entering into an agreement.

In addition to the seven sources described, there are many other ways to locate employment opportunities. The vehicles that are available to you depend upon your occupation. For example, data processing specialists and other technical businesses use various computer networks to list openings. There are computer networks for identifying many other types of occupations as well.

In addition, most professions have organizations that meet annually to promote membership, quality standards, and the sharing of information. The conferences are an excellent source for leads on job opportunities. Membership in the organization is usually required to attend such conferences, but it can be well worth it. The benefit of contacts usually far outweighs the minimal cost of membership.

Each state has an agency that offers employment services for most occupational levels and classifications. However, the services they offer typically assist people in lower paying occupations more than in the higher paying ones. These agencies usually offer some limited career counseling services, computerized career information services, and job listings. They also may offer screening services for employers who list openings with them. If you consider contacting these agencies, remember that it may take a long time before you see any results from your effort. Although these agencies can help, it is not a good idea to rely upon them as your sole source of opportunity.

You may also consider attending job fairs and career conferences. These events are often sponsored by university placement offices, employment agencies, or professional organizations. Normally they are advertised. Here, both employer representatives and job seekers are brought together in an informal atmosphere where they can meet, explore opportunities and interests, and set up formal interviews for a later time. Sometimes there is a low fee for either the employers or job seekers.

Additionally, many college and university placement offices offer their graduates access to job referral networks. Usually, such a referral is available for a nominal fee, although advice from such sources may cost you nothing. These offices usually have career counseling, lists of employers, career information centers, advice on resumes and interviews, and job listings available to their alumni. Not all schools offer such services, but it is worth investigating.

As you network, stay alert for advice regarding any other sources of opportunities. If it sounds good, investigate it!

Marketing Tips

1. Plan and apply your networking strategy carefully. It will probably be one of your best sources for identifying new opportunities.

2. When applying directly to organizations, try to identify a specific person inside the organization to contact. Establish the best way to apply for a position using this person's advice.

3. When responding to advertisements, use a carefully written cover letter, delay your response enough so it is more likely to receive attention, and keep a record of all ads to which you have responded.

4. When applying through open posting systems such as civil service, remember to be prepared for a lengthy waiting period on your application and processing. Plan accordingly by applying early in your job search.

5. If you contact recruiters or agencies, research them carefully to ensure your efforts will be worthwhile.

6. Remain alert during the entire job search to additional vehicles of employment opportunity and investigate them carefully.

Questions for Review

1. What is the most important part of your marketing campaign?

2. There are many ways to locate new employment opportunities in addition to direct application and responding to advertisements. Name four of them.

3. What is networking and upon what is it based?

4. Names for a *source list* can be developed from two primary groups. What are they?

5. What are the basic ingredients in a good cover letter?

6. Employment agencies fall into two general categories. What are they and what are the advantages and disadvantages of each?

7. There are three general types of recruiters; retainer, contingency, and corporate. Describe how they operate and how they are rewarded for their efforts.

Chapter Nine:
Interviewing
and Negotiating

We judge ourselves by what we feel capable of doing,
while others judge us by what we have already done.
Ralph Waldo Emerson

Making a Good Impression

Nothing has a greater impact on your chances for a successful career change than face-to-face interaction. Interviews provide you with the opportunity for this interaction. It is here that you must convince your potential employer that you are valuable. The impression you create in the interview is the single most important part of the employment process.

First impressions are critical. In fact, hiring decisions are often made within the first five to six minutes of the interview! Of course, this is not always the case; other factors affect the hiring decision too. Usually, candidates' resumes are screened carefully to identify those who have the proper work backgrounds and experience before an interview is granted. Additional screening and final decisions are then made during the interview process. Remember—the first in-person impression is extremely important!

Successful salary negotiations also require good interpersonal skills. These negotiations usually begin after an offer of employment is made. In their best seller, *Getting to Yes* (Boston: Houghton Mifflin Co., 1981), authors Roger Fisher and William Ury describe effective negotiation techniques. The authors emphasize the interpersonal side of the process:

> *A basic fact about negotiation, easy to forget in corporate and international transactions, is that you are dealing not with abstract representatives of the 'other side,' but with human beings . . . Failing to deal with others sensitively as human beings prone to human reactions can be disastrous for a negotiation.*

The interpersonal factors involved in interviewing and negotiating are known as **chemistry**. Good chemistry is essential to the interview and a significant part of salary negotiations. As you prepare for interviews and negotiations, it is important to draw heavily upon what you learned from the section on self-assessment, particularly regarding your interpersonal skills.

This does not mean that you should attempt to change your basic interpersonal style, but you should be aware of the impression you make on others. Be sensitive to the way others perceive you in interviewing and negotiating. This will help promote the proper chemistry between you and the potential employer.

Interviewing Techniques

Interviewing is often referred to as an art. This is because there are many different ways to create a positive impression. While there are basic skills and techniques to apply, your personal interpretation and application of these techniques will form the overall impression. No one style is necessarily any better than another. It is up to you to choose which style is best for you.

Everyone is different. Do not try to be someone you are not. If you are quiet and shy, do not try to become the *life of the party* simply to impress the interviewer. An outgoing personality is often an advantage in an interview, but not if you cannot live up to that image on your job. The best thing to do is to build upon the strengths of your style. You can do this by being aware of how your style can be an advantage. For example, if you have a serious personality, this may help you establish your image as a more predictable and consistent employee. Furthermore, since you know you tend to appear more serious, you can remember to *loosen up* a bit in the interview. Be yourself, but be flexible to fit the needs of the situation. Try to match or **complement** the interpersonal style of the interviewer. The ability to do this is known as a **people-skill**. People skills are abilities that help you get along with others.

The majority of today's careers call for people-skills. The ability to deal effectively with people at all levels leads to success in the business world. Concentrate on this in your interview. It can help create that all-important chemistry between you and the interviewer.

As you prepare for interviews, be aware that many of the people you are likely to interview with have not been professionally trained in interviewing techniques. As a result, their approaches will vary. However, three factors are almost certain to be addressed in any interview regardless of the background of the interviewer. Your **qualifications**, **interpersonal style**, and **interests** will always be at the heart of the interviewer's decision to hire you.

Qualifications

Qualifications refer to the work-related knowledge and skills a person must have to succeed in a new position. The proper qualifications are essential; they can get you an interview. However, if your qualifications do not meet the requirements, you will not get an offer.

Qualifications are established by your experience and education. You can do nothing to change them except obtain more experience and education. However, you *can* change the way you present them. Highlight and emphasize the most important facets of your experience that relate to the position for which you are interviewing. This is an essential technique in effective interviewing.

The interview will include discussion of your qualifications. This discussion supplements the information on your resume or application. While your resume should highlight your qualifications, your discussion in the interview must promote your strengths. Always try to gain as much information as possible about the organization and the position before you interview. Find out what the organization does and what type of image it projects. If you can learn something about your interviewer, do so.

One way to present your qualifications in a positive manner is to prioritize them before the interview. You will have some guidelines if you know the needs of the organization and the requirements of the position. Try to identify at least six important aspects of your experience, including education and achievements. Memorize them and be sure the interview does not end without the opportunity to discuss them at an appropriate time.

Never state your qualifications in a manner that cannot be factually supported! Always refer to them in a way that demonstrates your qualifications for the position. Above all, remember that it is best to let the interviewer draw these facts out of you. Letting the interviewer ask questions usually works better than a hard-sell approach. However, if the interviewer is not uncovering your qualifications, make sure you offer them in a tactful manner when appropriate. Remember—you may encounter an inexperienced interviewer. If this happens, be prepared to steer the conversation to the subjects that will highlight your qualifications before the end of the interview.

Interpersonal Style

As mentioned before, the first few minutes of the interview are often the ones that count the most. This is because we all tend to form immediate impressions of others by the way they appear as well as how they make us feel. Keep this in mind; it can be a tremendous advantage.

There is no one *best* way to make a good first impression. However, here are some ideas that will help you decide the best way for you to make a good first impression and improve the chemistry between you and your interviewer.

1. **First, remember that your nature cannot be altered radically.** You are unique. Therefore, strive to be yourself—your best self. You are most likely to be at your best if you are relaxed, prepared, and feel positive about the opportunity to interview. While there is almost always an element of tension in interviews, try not to let it bother you. Accept some degree of anxiety as natural, but focus more upon the information you want to exchange than the fact that you may be a little nervous.

2. **Preparation, especially regarding your qualifications and the questions you want to ask, will help make you more sure of yourself.** This technique will also provide you with a positive focus. Remember, you are there to learn about the position as well as help the interviewer learn why you are a good candidate for the opening.

3. **Good interpersonal style will lead the interviewer to like you.** One of the best ways to help someone like you is to make him or her feel liked. You can do this by appearing to be comfortable in his or her presence, listening attentively, and speaking with sincerity. This will give your interviewers the impression that you are

glad to have the opportunity to speak with them. Furthermore, your interviewer may be just as anxious to impress you. Try to make the interviewer feel as if he or she has succeeded in making a good impression.

4.   **Sometimes asking good questions can help you more than giving the *right* answers.** Well conceived questions about the organization, the nature of the position, the type of person they hope to hire, and other relevant considerations help convince the interviewer you understand what the position requires. Questions about the advantages of the position and organization as well as what the interviewer likes about working there, can actually help him or her sell you on the opportunity. Try to get the interviewer to promote the opportunity to you. It establishes a more positive impression of you in their mind.

5.   **Appropriate clothes and good grooming are vital!** Although most people know they should go to an interview looking their best, it is surprising how few actually know how to achieve this. Clean clothes are not enough. The choice of style and color are important as well as fit, posture, cleanliness, hairstyle, etc. If you can, find out what successful people in the company are wearing and base your appearance on this knowledge. It is usually best to dress conservatively for interviews, but in following these guidelines, don't be afraid to let your appearance reflect who you are. In some cases, showing some individual style may help you establish your identity in the eyes of the interviewer.

Awareness of interpersonal style will help you in the interview and in all phases of career success. Be sensitive to the impressions you convey as well as the messages others convey with their dress, facial expression, tone of voice, and body posture. Good interpersonal style will help you strengthen your ability to establish rapport and acceptance with your potential employer. This is one of your most powerful tools in reaching your career goals.

Interests

If a candidate is well qualified and has made a good impression on the interviewer(s), there are still some important questions that need to be answered. Will the candidate *fit* the position? Will the candidate relate well to his or her potential co-workers and superiors? Will the candidate be motivated by the rewards and challenges of the position? Will the candidate want to remain in the position, or is he or she likely to become bored and leave soon? Does the candidate's personality and value system fit with that of the employers? Do the candidate's interests match the unique work setting for which he or she is being considered?

Many candidates do not know how they compare with others on these issues because it is very difficult to evaluate the situation without inside knowledge about the organization, position, or people involved. It can be difficult, if not impossible, to obtain such information. However, you can strengthen your position by being sensitive to these issues.

Interests refer to the goals, values, and other factors that describe your characteristics and motivations. If your interests conflict with the nature of the position or the employer, you probably will not be hired. If your interests are in harmony with those of your employer, you are much more likely to fit in and be motivated to work; therefore, your chances of being hired are increased.

By describing your interests and learning more about the nature of the position, you will be in a position to promote yourself for the job if you want it. Remember—don't try to change your interests or your basic personality to fit a particular position. Even if you get hired, you will probably not be happy if you are trying to be someone you are not.

You will be able to promote yourself most effectively if you determine that your interests match the nature of the position. As you are being analyzed to see if you are a good match for the needs of the position, you can make your own analysis about the position. An important part of the whole process is to make sure being hired is good for both sides. It is flattering to be offered a job, but don't allow your ego to get in the way of common sense. If the position does not match your interests, do not pursue the opportunity. You may get into a situation which sets you back in your career path rather than ahead.

Preparing for the Interview

As you now know, if you want to make a good impression in your interview, you must do your homework. Here are some specific steps you can take to help prepare for it.

Before you interview:

1. **Read everything you can find about the organization.** Written material, such as public literature developed by the organization (annual reports, product brochures, reports to shareholders, promotional literature, etc.), and articles about the organization can give you a sense of the nature of the business issues the company faces.

2. **Talk to friends (or their contacts) who work in the organization.** Often, they can provide valuable information on events, policies, and people who may be very helpful to you.

3. **Be prepared to tell the interviewer why you are interested in the position.**

4. **Know your salary expectations.** Decide in advance the range of income you want, need, and will accept. Also determine when you will be able to begin work should you be offered an opportunity.

During the interview:
1. **Listen carefully to your interviewer.** The person who interviews you may offer revealing information if you ask the right questions and listen carefully for cues and key statements. It is usually acceptable to ask interviewers tactful questions about the challenges, issues, and potential frustrations that come with the position. Ask the interviewer what he or she likes about working in the organization.

2. **Keep your eyes and ears open.** When being introduced to potential co-workers, listen carefully to what they say about their jobs and the organization in general. Use **tact** and **discretion** to ask key questions that will help you determine the nature of the position. Try to remember the names of the people to whom you are introduced.

3. **Use every honest and practical resource available to learn about the nature of the opening and the organization.** This is as important as having the right qualifications and making an excellent impression.

Negotiations

If your qualifications, interpersonal style, and interests are right, you stand an excellent chance of receiving an offer. The offer is a turning point for you and the organization; both you and the other party hold something the other wants.

The ability to negotiate well when an offer of employment has been extended is critical to your long-term career success. Sometimes you may receive an offer of employment that does not include everything for which you had hoped. For example, the salary might not be as high as you had expected, certain benefits might be deleted, or other considerations such as starting date, moving expenses, etc. may not be satisfactory. Generally, it is normal to expect an offer that includes a 10% to 15% increase over your current range if you are being sought for a position. If you are seeking the position, an offer in your current range may be appropriate.

You do not have to accept an initial offer. Once an offer is extended to you, it will not be **rescinded** because you want to negotiate. It will only be rescinded when you ultimately do not accept the offer, or if you wait too long to make a decision.

There are some important rules to consider as you prepare for negotiations.

1. **Do not jump at any offer immediately, even if it sounds great.** Tell your potential employer that you would like to have some time to think about the offer. Find out how quickly they need to fill the position. Discuss the amount of time you will need to make the decision. Take enough time to think it over carefully and make a decision. Do you want to accept the offer; negotiate; or turn it down? Talk it over with your family and others you respect. Take the time to think carefully because your decision has long-term effects.

2. **Candidates who are good negotiators are realistic and flexible at the same time.** This means that although you may propose an **amendment** to the offer, you are not making a demand. Remember—negotiation means some measure of compromise or flexibility on both sides.

3. **Determine your bargaining position.** Analyze how much and how soon they need to fill that position. Think about salary, benefits, long-term opportunity, and all the other factors affecting the situation. Consider how difficult it may be for them to hire a back-up candidate behind you. Once you understand the strength or weakness of your position, you will be better prepared to develop your bargaining strategy.

4. **Decide whether or not you will ultimately accept the original offer or turn it down.** If you decide that you will ultimately turn it down unless they make some concessions, you are in a very strong position because you have nothing to lose by attempting to negotiate.

5. **Don't focus too much on compensation.** Consider all the factors that will be important to you before you make your decision. The factors that affect the total situation include compensation, long-term advancement opportunities, job satisfaction, your co-workers, how your family feels about the opportunity, whether a move is involved, cost of living, etc.

Once an offer is extended to you, your immediate response should almost always be, "Thank you very much. I am pleased to receive the offer. How long do I have until you need an answer?" This response indicates that you are very interested. It is also the first step in negotiations. Already you are beginning to negotiate the time frame in respect to how long you have before you must give an answer. If the recruiter or the employer reverses

the question and asks, "How long do you need?" you should have an answer prepared. Try to give yourself as much time as possible, but at the same time be realistic. Remember— they have a position that needs to be filled.

You will never be in a more powerful position with your potential employer than you are between the time the offer is extended, and the time that you accept or reject the offer. It is important that you understand this. It is very expensive, time consuming, and often frustrating for recruiters to find outstanding candidates. Once the recruiter or the employer has made an offer of employment, he or she is hoping very much that you will accept the position. In most cases, the recruiter will be willing to listen to your attempts at negotiating. If there is no flexibility in the offer, he or she will tell you. That is why it is important for you to make a decision prior to negotiations as to whether or not you will accept the offer as it stands, or ultimately decline it if amendments are not accepted.

The importance of enthusiasm in negotiations cannot be over-emphasized. Enthusiasm refers to the ability to make the other party believe you are interested in the position and that if you accept it you will be motivated to do well. Enthusiasm can be overdone; too much of it can work against you. However, the proper amount of enthusiasm increases the power of your position by making you a more attractive candidate. Remember, the recruiter or potential employer wants someone who is going to be highly motivated and who wants to do an outstanding job. During the negotiation stage, your enthusiasm indicates that you are more likely to be successful on the job if you take it.

Interviewing and Negotiating Tips

1. You only get one chance to make a good first
    impression. Plan your interview strategy carefully.
    The first impression in the interview often determines
    the ultimate outcome.

2. Always be yourself; but be your best self in the
    interview. This may mean flexing your style a little, but
    don't try to be something you are not.

3. Do your homework before the interview. Many career
    counselors believe that 70% of a person's interview effort
    should go into research prior to the interview, and 30%
    of the effort should go into the interview itself.

4. Pay close attention to your dress and physical
    appearance in all face-to-face discussions, whether you
    are interviewing or negotiating.

5. Effective negotiations require you to assess your degree
    of power before entering negotiations. Find out how
    badly they need you and how easily they can get
    another well-qualified candidate if you don't accept
    the offer as it is.

6. Be realistic and flexible in negotiations. This will
    encourage the other party to do the same.

7. Always demonstrate enthusiasm and interest. This will
    help convince the employer that you are someone for
    whom it is worthwhile to negotiate.

8. Your bargaining power is strongest between the time
    when the offer is extended and the time when you accept
    or reject the offer.

Questions for Review

1. What is the single most important part of the employment process?

2. What are the three major factors that are at the heart of an interviewer's decision to hire you?

3. Qualifications are established through experience and education. What other ingredient is essential for an effective interview?

4. What are the four specific steps you can take to prepare for an interview?

5. Name five important rules or guidelines you should consider as you prepare for negotiations.

6. When will you be in your most powerful position with your potential employer when negotiating for a job?

Epilogue

*If one advances confidently in the direction of
his dreams and endeavors to live the life he has
imagined, he will meet with success unexpected
in common hours.*

Henry David Thoreau

Making a career change is a very important decision. Such a change can benefit you greatly if you approach it in a responsible manner. Don't let the fear of a mid-life job change hinder your efforts to make the most of what can be a good opportunity. Focus on your strengths, your experience, and your maturity to reach your objective. Many factors besides competency can lead to success. As we have tried to point out in this book, the way you package your skills can make a world of difference. You must make yourself visible to the decision makers. Some job changers never quite succeed because they are not seen by the right people.

Too many people worry about things over which they have no control. Once you determine your objective, don't just sit around and think about it—do something about it! Concentrate on your objective and see it through to its conclusion.

Be assertive. Don't be reluctant to ask someone for advice, or to request an interview. *Let people know you have confidence in your abilities.*

Remember also, risk-taking is part of the mid-career change process. It is the risk-takers who make it in the job market. If you are confident that the risks you take will pay off and if you plan properly, you'll enjoy the success you seek.

At this point, you should be able to identify your values and your goals more clearly than ever before. You should also know more about yourself than ever before, and be able to relate that to your career objectives. *Applying this knowledge to plan for your success gives you control over your future!*

Remember—making a career change requires a positive attitude and the motivation to make a change. It is up to you to make the most of your potential.

Persistence and patience are also very important. Making
a mid-career change is not an easy task; but it can be
accomplished through calculated planning, persistence, and
patience. You are now on a fresh start to a new career. You
have a green light to move ahead, to build on your strengths,
and to focus on opportunity and a bright future.

Making a mid-career change requires a high level of commitment. Procrastination and failure to act are two of the biggest
reasons people fail in their effort to make a change.

Make use of all the sources available to you. People making
mid-career changes probably neglect this area the most.
Everyone has unlimited resources to explore in identifying job
opportunities. Take advantage of these resources and don't
limit yourself by not exploring all the avenues available. Most
people making a job change don't know how to make the best
use of the information available to them. Don't let this happen
to you!

As you make your career change, keep in mind that overall
quality of life is an important part of the equation. Economics
are also important, but don't lose sight of the quality of life you
seek when making your decision.

Finally, to succeed, you must want to succeed. Don't be
turned back from your goals when faced with adversity.
That's the mark of a winner.

Glossary of Terms

A

Activities – One's observable actions and behaviors.

Activities and accomplishments – Participation in events, other academics, or work; an optional heading on a resume.

Aesthetic – Visual appeal.

Aggressive – Assertive and active in pursuit of career goals.

Alienate – To offend or make hostile.

Amendment – A change or addition to a written document or verbal agreement.

Analysis – The study of something by breaking it down into smaller parts and looking at them carefully.

Aptitude test – An assessment instrument that helps determine a person's natural ability or capacity to learn.

B

Burn-out – An individual's loss of interest in a particular job or career path.

C

Career Goal – The ultimate, planned focus of a person's work experience.

Career objective – The type of work situation a person hopes to obtain.

Chemistry – A reaction that occurs as a result of the interaction of two or more people. The reactions are caused by the unique impressions individuals makes during interaction such as an interview.

Chronological format – Organization of job experience in the order of involvement on a resume.

Cold call – A call to a person one does not know.

Combination format – Categorization of job experience on a resume using a combination of functional and chronological approaches.

Communicative power – The level of influence within a specific written document.

Complement – To provide additional value or make complete.

Concise – Specific and brief.

Context – The circumstances that surround a specific occurrence or situation.

Contingency recruiters – Recruiters who are paid only when a job candidate they have referred is hired.

Contract employment – Work that is performed, usually within a set time period, for a pre-determined amount of compensation.

Corporate recruiters – Recruiters who are employed by a corporation and only work to find candidates for that organization.

Credentials – The experience and education a person has relative to a specific career path or position.

Credibility – The level of confidence that results from a person's word or actions.

Database – An electronic file of information or data.

Deterioration – The decline of an employment market for a particular job or occupational category.

Dilemma – A situation that involves a choice between two or more alternatives.

Discretion – To reason or use judgement prior to action.

Discriminate – To choose or reject a job candidate based upon factors that are irrelevant to his or her performance of the job.

Downsizing – Reducing the size of an organization's work force by permanent release of employees.

Education – The amount of formal training a person has received.

Embellishment – An addition that inflates one's qualifications.

Employability – The level of marketability of one's skills.

Employment experience – A person's work history.

Entrepreneur – A person who creates new business opportunities for profit.

Extraneous – External factors which have little bearing on an issue.

F

Functional format – Categorization of job experience according to job function on a resume.

G

General approach – A description of one's experience in a resume that does not emphasize a particular area of interest or experience.

Global economy – A condition in which worldwide economic forces influence local, regional, or national economics.

Global method – A general description of one's duties and responsibilities in each job on a resume.

Goals – Specific career or job related ambitions.

H

Harmony – Working well with others within a specific context.

Heading – The section of your resume that includes your name, address, and telephone number.

I

Illusion – Something that appears to be one way, when it is actually another; something that is deceiving.

Incentives – Rewards (monetary, promotional, verbal, etc.) received when goals are achieved.

Inevitable – A situation that cannot be avoided.

Interests – The things a person wants to do; One's preferred activities or objectives.

Interpersonal style – The pattern of behaviors that is unique to an individual.

Introspection – The examination of one's own thoughts and feelings.

J

Job bank – A listing of announcements regarding open positions.

Job market – The pool of jobs that are interesting to you; for which you are qualified; and which meet your goals in terms of situation, opportunity, and compensation.

L

Leisure – Activities outside work; rest and recreation.

Longevity – The length of time a person is employed in a specific position.

M

Mainstream – A primary information channel in a particular industry or business environment.

Marketable skills – Skills and abilities that are in demand in the employment market.

Materials logistics – Dealing with the procurement, maintenance and transport of materials.

Milestones – Important steps or achievements along a career path.

Motivation – A need or desire that causes a person to act.

N

Negotiate – To bargain for specific conditions of employment.

Networking – Making direct contacts to informed people in an industry.

Niche – The specific type of work a person is best fitted for and most motivated to do.

O

Objective self-assessment – Gathering facts about one's capabilities as well as shortcomings.

Objectives – Planned achievements; Specific achievements that are necessary to obtain a goal.

Obligations – Duties to which one is bound.

Obstacles – Things or people that stand in the way of progress.

Occupation specific job – A position that includes tasks and responsibilities that are normally a part of that position, regardless of the organization with which the person is employed.

Organization specific job – A position that includes tasks and responsibilities that are unique to the organization with which the person is employed.

Outline method – A basic sequential approach to provide limited information regarding one's qualifications.

Outplacement – A service that is designed to assist individuals in securing new employment.

P

People-skills – Skills that help a person get along well with others.

Periodical index – A source of information on accessing periodicals.

Personal data – Information that provides specific details about an individual, such as where they live and how they may be contacted.

Potential marketable skills – Skills which have not been used but that have value.

Plateau – To obtain a specific level of responsibility or achievement and remain there.

Plateauing – Reaching the highest level of achievement and no longer finding it challenging.

Prestige – Having the respect of your peers.

Priorities – To list items in order according to their level of importance.

Prioritize – To organize factors according the level of value they hold.

Priority – The level of value something holds.

Procrastinate – To delay action for little or no reason.

Procrastination – The delay of action for little or no reason.

Q

Qualifications – The specific abilities a person has regarding a particular need.

R

Rationalization – The explanations or reasons for one's actions or thoughts.

Reference directory – A directory of information on specific subjects.

References – Individuals who will attest to the abilities or competence of another person.

Regimentation – A high level of standardization or uniformity such as in a military organization.

Rescind – To take back an offer.

Retainer recruiters – Recruiters who are paid in increments during the course of an assignment.

S

Self-direction – Deliberate assessment and active planning regarding one's career path.

Skills assessment inventories – Tests that are designed to determine the level of competence in a specific skill area.

Skill gap – A deficiency in the skills that are necessary to perform a job or a type of job.

Sponsor – A person who recommends or assists another during an employment search.

Status – One's relative position in a hierarchy; the state of affairs.

Stigma – A poor impression that is related to a person or thing, often without any real cause.

Subjective – Judgements or opinions that are influenced by personal considerations.

Supply/demand ratio – The level of availability of a particular commodity (or labor pool) relative to the level of demand.

T

Tact – The ability to demonstrate sensitivity toward others during interpersonal relations; a people-skill.

Tactile – Able to be felt by the sense of touch.

Targeted approach – A method of organizing information in a way that highlights or emphasizes certain duties, activities, or qualifications on a resume.

Task specific method – Writing a resume in a fashion that highlights or emphasizes certain duties or activities.

Trade publications – Magazines or periodicals related to a specific occupation.

U

Underemployment – The condition that exists when a person works in a position that requires (and generally pays) less than he or she is capable of doing (or earning).

W

Written plan – A course of action that is written down.

Note: Adapted from *Webster's New Collegiate Dictionary*. (G. & C. Merriam and Co., 1976)

APPENDIX A
DIRECTORIES

(For Leads to Potential Employers and
Sources of Employer Information)

DIRECTORIES
(Business and Financial)

The Directory of Corporate Affiliations
National Register Publishing
Company (A subsidiary of Reed
Reference Publications)
P.O. Box 31
New Providence, NJ 07974
800/521-8110

- Profiles of over 4,000 U.S. companies, includes subsidiaries, divisions, and affiliates
- A handy way to trace a company back to its parent company.

Directories in Print
Gale Research Company
Book Tower
Detroit, MI 48226
313/961-2242

- Lists about 8,000 directories, both general and industry-specific.
- Listed by industry, also geographically indexed.

Directory of Management Consultants
Consultant News
Templeton Road
Fitzwilliam, NH 03447
603/585-2200

- Lists firm, address, phone numbers, contact person, etc.

Dun's Million Dollar Directory
Dun & Bradstreet
3 Sylvan Way
Parsippamy, NJ 07054
800/526-0651

- Lists 160,000 U.S. businesses in a variety of industries, including utilities, industrial, transportation, banking, finance; classified alphabetically, by industry, and geographically.
- Listings include name, address, phone number, top executives' names and titles, financial statistics, accounting firm, principal bank, and more.

Dun's Top 50,000 Companies
Dun & Bradstreet
3 Sylvan Way
Parsippamy, NJ 07054
800/526-0651

- The top 50,000 companies of the 160,000 listed in the *Million Dollar Directory*.
- As above, listings include address, phone number, executive names and titles, and stats.

Dun & Bradstreet's Reference Book of Corporate Managements
Dun & Bradstreet
3 Sylvan Way
Parsippamy, NJ 07054
800/526-0651

- Brief biographies of executives – including CEOs, CFOs, directors, presidents and vice-presidents of top U.S. companies.
- Profiles include business address and phone number, title, employment history, education, clubs and memberships, civic and political activities, awards and honors received.

Encyclopedia of Associations
Gale Research Company
Book Tower
Detroit, MI 48226
313/961-2242

- Published in several volumes; the most useful is *Trade & Professional Associations*, which lists over 20,000 associations alphabetically by industry.
- Also indexed by name, geographic locations and executive names (special volume for cross-indexing purposes).
- An excellent kick-off point for networking.
- Also available on-line in DIALOG.

Guide to American Directories
B. Klein Publications
P.O. Box 8503
Coral Springs, FL 33075
305/752-1708

- Similar to the above, but less extensive, this directory lists over 7,000 directories indexed by subject.
- Of special interest: under Manufacturers heading, lists industrial directories for each state.

Moody's Industrial Manual
Moody's Investor Service, Inc.
99 Church Street
New York, NY 10013
212/553-0300

- Lists 3,000 companies listed on the New York or American Stock Exchanges as well as international companies.
- Includes address, phone number and statistics (Moody's also publishes directories for Bank & Finance, Public Utilities, Transportation, Municipals).

Polk City Directory
R.L. Polk & Company
P.O. Box 305100
Nashville, TN 37230-5100
615/889-3350

- By city, lists names and titles of local executives with brief explanation of their companies.

Standard & Poor's Register of Corporations, Directors and Executives
Standard & Poor's Corporation
25 Broadway
New York, NY 10004
212/208-8000

- Lists over 45,000 U.S. corporations; includes names and titles of over 400,000 corporate officials, corporation's principal bank and law firm.
- Of special interest: Volume 2 contains biographies of 75,000 executives and directors, includes business and home addresses, date and place of birth, and organization/ association memberships.

Standard Directory of Advertisers
Reed Reference Publishing, Co.
P.O. Box 31
New Providence, NJ 07974
800/521-8110

- Lists about 17,000 companies that place national and/or regional advertising (not a listing of ad agencies).
- Of special interest: each listing includes names and titles of management, financial, advertising, and marketing executives.
- An excellent one-stop reference for a resume mailing list.

Thomas Register
Thomas Publishing Company
One Pennsylvania Plaza
New York, NY 10013
212/695-0500

- 12-volume directory of U.S. manufacturers; Volumes 1-6 contain alphabetical listing of products/services; Volume 7, brand names only.
- Volume 8 is an alphabetical listing of U.S. manufacturers, including name, address, phone number, product lines, executives, branches, representatives, and distributors.
- Also available on-line on DIALOG.

PERIODICALS

Barron's National Business and Financial Weekly
Dow Jones & Company, Inc.
22 Cortlandt Street
New York, NY 10007
212/285-5243

- Widely-read business/ investments/finance newspaper.
- First section contains articles and columns on news, industry trends, and recent developments; second section contains stock tables and statistics.

Business Week
McGraw-Hill, Inc.
1221 Avenue of the Americas
New York, NY 10020
212/997-1221

Special issues include:
- Corporate Scoreboard Issue (March), which lists about 1,200 top companies in business, industrial, and financial categories.
- Bank Scoreboard Issue (April), which ranks the 200 largest U.S. banks.

Forbes
Forbes, Inc.
60 Fifth Avenue
New York, NY 10011
212/620-2200

Special issues include:
- Annual Report on American Industry (January), which lists about 1,000 top industrial firms; listings include name, sales profit, growth rate, etc.
- 500 Largest Corporations (mid-May) ranked by revenue, profits, assets, stock value, etc.

Fortune
Time, Inc.
Rockefeller Cemter
Time & Life Building
New York, NY 10020
212/522-1212

Special issues include:
- 500 Largest U.S. Corporations (May).
- Second 500 Largest U.S. Corporations (June).
- 50 Largest Commercial Banks, Life Insurance, Utilities, Retail, Financial Services, and Transportation Companies (July).

International Management
McGraw-Hill, Inc.
1221 Avenue of the Americas
New York, NY 10020
212/512-2000

- Management strategies, trends, developments, and techniques.

**COMPUTER DATABASES
(General Information and
Financial)**

D&B—Dun's Financial Records
Dun's Marketing Services
Sylvan Way
Parsippany, NJ 07054
201/455-0900

- Information on over 700,000 companies, including balance sheets, history, comparisons with competitors, and more.
- Available on DIALOG

D&B—Dun's Market Identifiers
Dun's Marketing Services
Sylvan Way
Parsippany, NJ 07054
201/455-0900

- Directory of over two million U.S. private and public companies with earnings over $1 million, or employing ten or more people.
- Profiles include address, financial statistics, names and titles of executives.
- Available on DIALOG.

D&B—Million Dollar Directory
Dun's Marketing Services
Sylvan Way
Parsippany, NJ 07054
201/455-0900

- Lists 160,000 businesses in a variety of industries, incl. utilities, industrial, banking, transportation, finance; all with earnings over $500,000.
- Listings include name, address, phone number, top executives' names and titles, financial statistics, accounting firm, principal bank, and more.
- Available on DIALOG.

Disclosure On-line
Disclosure, Inc.
5161 River Road
Bethesda, MD 20816
301/951-1300

- Profiles of over 10,000 publicly-held companies that file with the Securities Exchange Commission.
- Extensive information includes 10k's, income statements, stockholder's reports, and more.
- Available on CompuServe, DIALOG, Dow Jones News/Retrieval, I.P. Sharp, ISYS, Quotron, Warner Computer Systems.

Management Contents
Information Access Company
362 Lakeside Drive
Foster City, CA 94404
800/227-8431

- Abstracts of articles from over 7,000 business publications, including technical journals, newsletters, reports, and much more.
- Available on DIALOG, SDC, BRS, Data-Star, The Source.

Moody's Corporate News—U.S.
Moody's Investor Services, Inc.
99 Church Street
New York, NY 10007
212/553-0300

- Up-to-date business news on over 13,000 publicly-held companies, including manufacturers, utilities, savings & loan associations, banks, real estate firms, and more.
- Weekly updates with news culled from leading magazines and newspapers, newswire services, stock exchange reports, annual reports, quarterly earning statements, press releases, prospectuses, and other sources.
- Available on DIALOG.

Moody's Corporate Profiles
Moody's Investor Services, Inc.
99 Church Street
New York, NY 10007
212/553-0300

- Profiles of companies traded
  on the New York and
  American Stock Exchanges,
  as well as most active o-t-c
  companies · about 3,600
  companies total.
- As above, weekly updates
  from a wide variety of
  sources.
- Profiles include extensive
  financial information.
- Available on DIALOG.

PTS Annual Reports Abstracts
Predicasts, Inc.
11001 Cedar Avenue
Cleveland, OH 44106
800/321-6388

- Predicasts on-line, with
  abstracts dating back to
  1982 and information on
  over 3,000 publicly held
  companies.
- Information from annual
  reports, 10k statements.
- Available on DIALOG, BRS,
  BRS/BRKTHRU, Data-Star.

PTS Promt
Predicasts, Inc.
11001 Cedar Avenue
Cleveland, OH 44106
800/321-6388

- Abstracts from top business
  publications covering over
  120,000 national and
  international companies.
- Available on BRS, Data-Star,
  DIALOG, VU/TEXT.

*Standard & Poor's Corporate
Descriptions*
Standard & Poor's Corporation
25 Broadway
New York, NY 10004
212/208-8000

- Profiles on over 8,000
  publicly-held U.S.
  corporations.
- Available on DIALOG.

Trade & Industry ASAP
Information Access Company
362 Lakeside Drive
Foster City, CA 94404
800/227-8431

- Full text from over 100
  business and trade
  magazines (such as *American
  Banker*, *Chain Store Age*,
  Advertising Age, *Women's
  Wear Daily* and other top
  industry publications); also
  includes top business
  magazines such as *Forbes*,
  Fortune, *Dun's Business
  Month* and *Money*.
- Available on DIALOG.

RECRUITING ACCESS

Career Placement Registry
302 Swann Avenue
Alexandria, VA 22301
800/368-3093

- Resume-listing service; resume is listed for six months, a year for college seniors.
- Cost is minimal—from $12 for students to $45 for people in the $40,000 + salary range.
- Roughly 400 companies a month request resumes.

Delphi
General Videotex Corporation
1030 Massachusetts Avenue
Cambridge, MA 02138
800/544-4005

- A popular system that offers a combination service listing both situation-wanted and help-wanted ads.
- For a one time $49.95 fee, you can place an ad and browse through openings.
- A wide area of fields covered, including: finance, sales and marketing, hotel/restaurant management, engineering.

On-line Careers
Information Intelligence, Inc.
P.O. Box 31098
Phoenix, AZ 85046
800/228-9982

- Lists job categories in the information systems field.

APPENDIX B
RESOURCE INFORMATION
ON THE RECRUITING INDUSTRY

**The Association of Executive
Search Consultants**
230 Park Avenue, Ste. 1549
New York, NY 10169
Telephone: (212) 949-9556

The Association of Executive
Search Consultants, founded
in 1959, is the best-known
professional group in the industry. About sixty retainer-search
firms belong. The Association's
membership directory includes a
code of ethics and professional
practice guidelines.

Executive Search System
Custom Databanks, Inc.
13925 Esworthy Road
Germantown, MD 20874-3313
Telephone: (301) 990-4010

For those who own a computer,
there is *The Executive Search
System*, a database program that
contains information about
approximately 1,500 executive-
search firms. The program allows
you to target a subset of search
firms based on industry specialty,
position or functional specialty,
minimum salary of positions
handled, geographical location,
whether the firm is retainer or
contingency, and so on. You can
print envelopes, mailing labels,
and cover letters based on information from the program. The
database is updated regularly
and costs $75.

Kennedy & Kennedy, Inc.
*Directory of Executive
Recruiters*
Templeton Road
Fitzwilliam, NH 03447
Telephone: (603) 585-2200

This publication provides reference to over 1,800 recruiting
firms including names of recruiters, addresses, specialty areas
and related information. It also
includes additional information
on how to use recruiters to your
advantage.

Kennedy & Kennedy, Inc.
Consultants News
Templeton Road
Fitzwilliam, NH 03447
Telephone: (603) 585-2200

An annually updated directory of
executive recruiters, containing
names of about 2,000 firms.
Kennedy also publishes *Executive
Recruiter News*, a widely read
industry newsletter. Its target
audience is recruiters, not job
seekers, but it will give anyone
interested in the field an insider's
view of the industry. In addition
to his Directory, each year
Kennedy selects a list of what
he considers to be the country's
leading fifty search firms.

Kenneth J. Cole
The Recruiting and Search Report
P.O. Box 9433
Panama City Beach, FL 32407
Telephone: (904) 235-3733

Kenneth J. Cole publishes a variety of directories useful to the job seeker. He offers a series of about 60 separate lists of recruiting firms, focusing on specific industries, functions, specialty areas, or types of firms. They are updated approximately three times a year. Another publication, *Independent Researchers and Services*, provides a listing of independent researchers. He also publishes a quarterly newsletter, *The Recruiting and Search Report*.

The National Association of Executive Recruiters
J.H. Dugan Associates
225 Crossroads Boulevard
Carmel, CA 93923
Telephone: (408) 625-5880

The National Association of Executive Recruiters, with approximately 100 member firms, contains both retainer and contingency firms.

The National Association of Personnel Consultants
3133 Mt. Vernon Avenue
Alexandria, VA 22305
Telephone: (703) 684-0180

The National Association of Personnel Consultants publishes a *Career Guide Handbook*, which includes a membership list divided by specialty. This list does not distinguish between executive search firms and employment agencies, however, except for a short listing of retainer firms.

APPENDIX C
RECRUITING FIRMS

RETAINER

The following retainer firms make placements in a variety of industries. The largest ones cover just about every industry or function. The smaller firms may confine themselves to a narrower focus.

Battalia & Associates
Contact Person: O. William Battalia
275 Madison Avenue
New York, NY 10016
212/683-9440

Bowden & Co., Inc.
Contact Person: Otis Bowden II
5000 Rockside Road, #120
Cleveland, OH 44131
216/447-1800

Boyden International
Contact Person: Putney Westerfield
375 Park Avenue, Ste. 1008
New York, NY 10152
212/685-3400
Note: Additional offices in Atlanta, FL; Boston, MA; Chicago, IL; Cleveland, OH; Dallas, TX; Ft. Lauderdale, FL; Houston, TX; Los Angeles, CA; Menlo Park, CA; Morristown, NJ; Pittsburgh, PA; San Francisco, CA; Stamford, CT; Washington, DC; and abroad.

Canny, Bowen, Inc.
Contact Person: Patricia McCauley
200 Park Avenue, 4th Floor
New York, NY 10166
212/949-6611
Note: Additional office in Boston.

Christenson & Montgomery
Contact Person: Robert M. Montgomery
466 Southern Boulevard
Chatham, NJ 07928
201/966-1600

Thorndike Deland Associates
Contact Person: Howard Bratches
275 Madison Avenue
New York, NY 10016
212/661-6200

Robert W. Dingman Company, Inc.
Contact Person: R.W. Dingman
32129 W. Lindero Canyon Road
West Lake Village, CA 91361
818/991-5950

Fleming Associates
Contact Person: Dick Fleming
1428 Franklin Street
Columbus, IN 47201
812/376-9061
Note: Additional offices in Atlanta, GA; Des Moines, IA; Austin, TX; Louisville, KY; Metairie, LA; Sarasota, FL; Stamford, CT.

Gilbert Tweed Associates
Contact Person: Janet Tweed
630 Third Avenue
New York, NY 10017
212/697-4260
Note: Additional offices in
Boston, MA; Winterport, ME;
and Washington, DC.

Garofolo Curtiss & Co.
Contact Person: Frank Garofolo
326 W. Lancaster Avenue
Ardmore, PA 19003
215/896-5080
Note: Additional offices in
Boston, MA; Camp Hill, PA;
Naperville, IL; Nashville, TN;
Ponte Vedra Beach, FL; and
Washington, DC.

Goodrich & Sherwood
Contact Person: Saul Samet
521 Fifth Avenue
New York, NY 10175
212/697-4131

Gould & McCoy
Contact Person: William Gould
300 Park Avenue, 20th Floor
New York, NY 10022
212/688-8671

Handy Associates
Contact Person: Gerald Simmons
250 Park Avenue
New York, NY 10177
212/557-0400

Haskell & Stern
Contact Person: Allan D.R. Stern
380 Madison Avenue, 7th Floor
New York, NY 10017
212/856-4451

The Heidrick Partners, Inc.
Contact Person: Robert L.
Heidrick
20 North Wacker Drive, #2850
Chicago, IL 60606
312/845-9700

Heidrick & Struggles, Inc.
Contact Person: David R.
Peasback
245 Park Avenue
New York, NY 10167
212/867-9876
Note: Additional offices in
Atlanta, GA; Boston, MA;
Chicago, IL; Cleveland, OH;
Dallas, TX; Greenwich, CT;
Houston, TX; Los Angeles, CA;
Menlo Park, CA; San Francisco,
CA; and Washington, DC.

Hodge-Cronin & Associates
Contact Person: Richard J.
Cronin
9575 West Higgins Road
Rosemont, IL 60018
708/692-2041

Ward Howell International
Contact Person: Max Ulrich
99 Park Avenue
New York, NY 10016
212/697-3730
Note: Additional offices in
Chicago, IL; Dallas, TX;
Greenwich, CT; Houston, TX;
Los Angeles, CA; San Francisco,
CA; and abroad.

Johnson Smith & Knisely, Inc.
Contact Person: Sheri Pearlman
475 Fifth Avenue
New York, NY 10017
212/686-9760

A. T. Kearney, Inc.
Contact Person: James R. Arnold
222 West Adams
Chicago, IL 60606
312/648-0111
Note: Additional offices in
Atlanta, GA; Denver, CO; Los
Angeles, CA; Miami, FL; New
York, NY; and Scottsdale, AZ.

Korn/Ferry International
Contact Person: Howard S.
Freedman
237 Park Avenue
New York, NY 10017
212/687-1834
Note: Additional offices in Los
Angeles, CA; Atlanta, GA; Boston;
Chicago, IL; Cleveland, OH;
Dallas, TX; Denver, CO; Houston,
TX; Minneapolis, MN; Newport
Beach, CA; Palo Alto, CA; San
Francisco, CA; Seattle, WA;
Stamford, CT; Washington, DC;
and abroad.

Lamalie Associates, Inc.
Contact Person: William G. Long
498 Fifth Avenue, 14th Floor
New York, NY 10017
212/953-7900
Note: Additional offices in
Atlanta, GA; Chicago, IL;
Cleveland, OH; Dallas, TX; and
Tampa, FL.

R. H. Larsen & Associates
Contact Person: Robert H. Larsen
1401 E. Broward Boulevard,
Ste. 101
Ft. Lauderdale, FL 33301
305/763-9000

Nordeman Grimm, Inc.
Contact Person: Peter Grimm
717 Fifth Avenue
New York, NY 10022
212/758-2300
Note: Additional office in Chicago.

The Ogdon Partnership
Contact Person: Thomas H.
Ogdon
375 Park Avenue
New York, NY 10152
212/308-1600

Peat Marwick Main & Co.
Contact Person: Donald F. Dvorak
303 E. Wacker Drive
Chicago, IL 60601
312/938-1000
Note: Additional offices in
Atlanta, GA; Boston, MA; Dallas,
TX; Denver, CO; Hartford, CT;
Houston, TX; Los Angeles, CA;
Miami, FL; Minneapolis, MN;
Newport Beach, CA; New York,
NY; San Francisco, CA; and
Stamford, CT.

Network Affiliates
Contact Person: Michael R.
Wagner
1101 Veterans Blvd., Suite. #6
Kenner, LA 70062
504/461-5511
Note: executive level recruiting
services for all industries.

Paul R. Ray & Company, Inc.
Contact Person: Paul R. Ray
301 Commerce Street, #2300
Ft. Worth, TX 76102
817/334-0500
Note: Additional offices in
Atlanta, GA; Chicago, IL; Dallas,
TX; Houston, TX; New York, NY;
and Los Angeles, CA.

Russell Reynolds Associates
Contact Person: Richard S.
Lannamann
200 Park Avenue, 23rd Floor
New York, NY 10166
212/351-2000
Note: Additional offices in Boston,
MA; Chicago, IL; Dallas; Los
Angeles, CA; Stamford, CT;
Cleveland, OH; Washington, DC;
Houston, TX; Minneapolis, MN;
San Francisco, CA; and abroad.

**Sydney Reynolds Associates
Inc.**
Contact Person: Sydney Reynolds
342 Madison Avenue, Ste. 2001
New York, NY 10173
212/697-8682

Ropes Associates, Inc.
Contact Person: John Ropes
333 North New River Drive East
Suite 4000
Ft. Lauderdale, FL 33301
305/525-6600

Susan Shultz & Associates
Contact Person: Susan Shultz
4350 East Camelback Road,
Suite. 200
Phoenix, AZ 85018
602/948-7214

Slayton International, Inc.
Contact Person: Dick Slayton
181 West Madison Street,
Suite 4510
Chicago, IL 60602
312/456-0080

Spencer Stuart & Associates
Contact Person: Thomas Neff
55 East 52nd Street
New York, NY 10055
212/407-0200
Note: Additional offices in
Atlanta, GA; Chicago, IL; Dallas,
TX; Houston, TX; Los Angeles,
CA; Philadelphia, PA; San
Francisco, CA; and Stamford, CT.

Sheila Wolf Associates
Contact Person: Sheila Wolf
300 East 75th Street #23A
New York, NY 10021
212/517-7398

**Egon Zehnder International,
Inc.**
55 East 59th Street
New York, NY 10022
212/838-9199
Note: International firm
headquartered in Switzerland;
additional U.S. offices in Atlanta,
GA; Los Angeles, CA; and
Chicago, IL.

APPENDIX D
SPECIALTY RECRUITING FIRMS

RETAINER AND CONTINGENCY

The following firms specialize in a particular industry or function. Some work exclusively by retainer; others do both contingency and retainer searches.

AD AGENCY/MEDIA/PR

Bornholdt Shivas & Friends
Contact Person: John Bornholdt
295 Madison Avenue #1206
New York, NY 10017
212/557-5252

Jerry Fields Associates
Contact Person: Jerry Fields
353 Lexington, 11th Floor
New York, NY 10016
212/661-6644

Plaza, Inc.
Contact Person: Ellen Kirk
55 East Monroe #3834
Chicago, IL 60603
312/263-0944

ADMINISTRATION

Joe C. Malone Associates
Conact Person: Joe Malone
1941 Bishop Lane
Louisville, KY 40218
502/456-2380

APPAREL/TEXTILE

Colton, Bernard Inc.
Contact Person: Roy C. Colton
870 Market Street, Ste. 822
San Francisco, CA 94102
415/399-8700

Robert Howe & Associates
Contact Person: Robert W. Hamill
35 Glenlake Parkway, Ste. 164
Atlanta, GA 30328
404/390-0030

Jaral Fashion Personnel Consultants
Contact Person: Joseph Morgan
443 Springfield Avenue
Summitt, NJ 07901
908/273-1110

ARCHITECTURE/DESIGN

Corporate Builders
Contact Person: Bill Meysing
812 S. W. Washington Street,
Ste. 850
Portland, OR 97251
503/223-4344

Design Executive Search
Contact Person: Rita Sue Siegel
18 E. 48th Street, 18th Floor
New York, NY 10017
212/308-0700

ASSOCIATION MANAGEMENT/ NONPROFIT

Development Search Specialists
Contact Person: Fred J.
Lauerman
W1072 First National Bank
Building
St. Paul, MN 55101
612/224-3750

Ketchum, Inc.
Contact Person: Calvin H.
Douglas
1030 Fifth Avenue
Pittsburgh, PA 15219
412/281-1481

Robison & McAuley
Contact Person:
John H. Robison
128 S. Tyrone Street, Ste. 1350
Charlotte, NC 28202
704/376-0059

BANKING/FINANCIAL SERVICES

TBR Group, Ltd.
The Bankers Register
Contact Person: Howard Stevens
500 Fifth Avenue
New York, NY 10110
212/840-0800

Watkins & Associates
Contact Person: Michael Watkins
7322 Southwest Freeway #620
Houston, TX 77074
713/777-5261

BROKERAGE/SECURITIES

Corporate Search Inc.
Contact Person: Don Fouracre
16291 W. Fourteen Mile, Ste. 24
Birmingham, MI 48025
313/644-7730

Cadillac Associates/Search
Specialists
Contact Person: Dwight Hanna
1005 Sunrise Way, Ste. 353
Palm Springs, CA 92262
619/327-0920

CHEMICAL

Fred Anthony Associates
Contact Person: Fred Anthony
P.O. Box 372
Lake Geneva, WI 53147
414/248-8133

Larson Associates
Contact Person: Ray Larson
P.O. Box 9005
Brea, CA 92621
714/529-4121

Merlin International
Contact Person: Henry Keller
P.O. Box 313
Ramsey, NJ 07446
201/825-7220

COMPUTER INDUSTRY/EDP

EDP Consultants, Inc.
Contact Person: Ron Anderson
P.O. Box 26066
Milwaukee, WI 53226
414/476-3335

Innovative Resources
Corporation
Contact Person: Joseph Greco
Beachcliff Executive Center
1340 Depot Street, Ste. 210
Rocky River, OH 44116
216/331-1757

DIRECT MARKETING

Ridenour & Associates
Contact Person: Suzanne
Ridenour
One E. Walker Drive, Ste. 3500
Chicago, IL 60601
312/644-1888

VanReypen Enterprises, Ltd.
Contact Person: Robert D.
VanReypen
3100 Monroe Avenue
Rochester, NY 14618
716/586-8014

ENGINEERING

Aim Executive, Inc.
Contact Person: Jeff DePerro
6605 West Central Avenue
Toledo, OH 43617
419/841-5040

Headhunters National, Inc.
Contact Person: Beverly Bachand
5319 SW Westgate Drive
Portland, OR 97221
503/297-1451

Search Enterprises, Inc.
Contact Person: Jim Sullivan
520 Quail Ridge Drive
Westmont, IL 60559
708/654-2300

Sharrow & Associates
Contact Person: Douglas
Sharrow
24735 Van Dyke
Centerline, MI 48015
313/759-6910

FINANCE/ACCOUNTING

Joy Reed Belt & Associates
Contact Person: Joy Reed
Belt, Ph.D.
P.O. Box 18446
Oklahoma City, OK 73154
405/842-6336

Upper Midwest, Inc.
Contact Person: Floyd
Robertson
12 South Sixth Street #626
Minneapolis, MN 55402
612/338-6748

FOOD/BEVERAGE

Image Support Systems
Contact Person: Wallace A. Smith
1929 Cable Street
San Diego, CA 92107
619/226-1146

J. Lee & Associates
Contact Person: Judy Lee
P.O. Box 16634
Panama City, FL 32406
904/763-8285

Unique, Specialty Group, Inc.
Contact Person: Jennifer B. Flora
8765 N. Guion Road
Ste. A
Indianapolis, IN 46268
317/875-8281

HEALTH INDUSTRY

Hospital Staffing Services, Inc.
Contact Person: Jay Gershberg
6245 N. Federal Hwy, Ste. 500
Ft. Lauderdale, FL 33308
305/771-0500

Jonas Position Services
Contact Person: Glenn Jonas
3720 N. 124th Street, Ste. O
Milwaukee, WI 53222
414/466-4666

Joslin & Associates, Ltd.
Contact Person: Robert S.
Joslin, Ph.D.
291 Deer Trail Court, Ste. C
Barrington, IL 60010
708/382-7778

Witt and Associates, Inc.
Contact Person: John Witt
2015 Spring Road
Oak Brook, IL 60521
708/574-5070
Note: Another office in Dallas.

HIGH TECHNOLOGY

The Leslie Corporation
Contact Person: John Leslie
10700 N. Freeway, Ste. 370
Houston, TX 77037
713/591-0915

Storti Associates
Contact Person: Michael Storti
4060 Post Road
Warwick, RI 02886
401/885-3100

INSURANCE

Errol Houk Associates
Contact Person: April Houk
6209 Constitution Drive
Ft. Wayne, IN 46804
219/432-7666

LEGAL

Howard C. Bloom Company
Contact Person: Howard Bloom
5000 Quorum, Suite 160
Dallas, TX 75240
214/385-6455

Kanarek & Shaw
Contact Person: Carol M.
Kanarek
301 East 53rd Street
New York, NY 10022
212/371-0967

MANUFACTURING/ OPERATIONS

The Borton Wallace Company
Contact Person: Murray B.
Parker
22 Broad Street
Asheville, NC 28801
704/252-5831

MANAGEMENT INFORMATION SERVICES

Bay Search Group
Contact Person: Ford K. Sayre
90 Elm Street
Providence, RI 02903
401/751-2870

John J. Davis Associates
Contact Person: John J. Davis
521 Fifth Ave., Ste. 1740
New York, NY 10175
212/286-9489

PACKAGING

Grantham & Company, Inc.
Contact Person, John D.
Grantham
207 Providence
Chapel Hill, NC 27514
919/489-1991

PERSONNEL/HUMAN RESOURCES

J.R. Brody & Associates
Contact Person: James R. Brody
P.O. Box 1421
Summit, NJ 07902-8421
908/522-0450

Romeo-Hudgins & Associates,
Inc.
Contact Person: Paul C. Romeo
900 East Eighth Avenue, #300
King of Prussia, PA 19406
215/768-8002

Charles Russ Associates, Inc.
Contact Person: Charles F.
Russ, Jr.
P.O. Box 667
Shawnee Mission, KS 66206-
0667
913/338-1211

R&D

The Executive Search Group
Contact Person: E.R. Bower
P.O. Box 740576
Dallas, TX 75374
214/690-1179

Jim King & Associates
Contact Person: Jim King
1301 Gulf Life Drive, Ste. 1901
Jacksonville, FL 32207
904/398-7371

REAL ESTATE

Continental Search Associates,
Inc.
Contact Person: William Dewey
P.O. Box 413
Birmingham, MI 48012
313/644-4506

Huey Enterprises
Contact Person: Arthur Huey
273 Clarkson Exeuctive Park
Ellisville, MO 63011
314/394-9393

RETAIL/HOSPITALITY

Michael Kosmetos & Associates
Contact Person: Michael
Kosmetos
333 Babbitt Road, Ste. 3001
Cleveland, OH 44123
216/261-1950

SALES & MARKETING

Sales Executives, Inc.
Contact Person: Dale E. Statson
755 W. Big Beaver Road, #2107
Troy, MI 48084
313/362-1900

Joel Wilensky Associates
Contact Person: Joel H. Wilensky
P.O. Box 155
Sudbury, MA 01776
508/443-5176

TELECOMMUNICATIONS

Richard Farber Associates
Contact Person: Richard Farber
60 Cutter Mill Road
Great Neck, NY 11021
516/627-6090

Xagas & Associates
Contact Person: Steve Xagas
701 East State Street
Geneva, IL 60134
708/232-7044

APPENDIX E
SUGGESTED READING

Allen, Jeffrey G. *How to Turn an Interview Into a Job.* Simon & Schuster, Inc., New York, NY, 1983.

A practical, how to system for interviewing, follow-up, and related considerations. Appropriate for entry level through management positions.

Bolles, Richard N. *What Color is Your Parachute?* Ten Speed Press, Berkeley, CA, 1989.

This is a classic on job seeking. Bolles offers a strategy for conducting a job campaign that challenges traditional methods. An annotated bibliography is included as an appendix. This bibliography lists by category books that are relevant to job changes.

Bostwick, Burdette E. *Resume Writing.* John Wiley and Sons, Inc., New York, NY, 1985.

This book includes a discussion on different types of resumes as well as many examples. Also includes exercises to assist the reader in assessing his experience in order to relate to corporate needs.

Cohn, Steve and Paulo de Oliveira. *Getting to the Right Job.* Workman Publishing, New York, NY, 1987.

Provides excellent guidance for college graduates searching for their first professional position. Includes comprehensive information on identification of opportunities, interviewing, college recruitment and negotiations.

Cole, Diane. *Hunting the Headhunters: A Woman's Guide.* Simon & Schuster, Inc., New York, NY, 1987.

Well-written advice for both women and men. This book provides good perspective on a variety of recruiting professionals and how to contact as well as respond to them when looking for new job opportunities.

Covey, Stephan R. *The Habits of Highly Effective People.* Simon & Schuster, Inc., New York, NY, 1989.

A principle-centered approach for solving personal and professional problems.

Davison, Roger. *You Can Get Anything You Want.* Simon & Schuster, New York, NY, 1987.

This book provides basic principles of negotiations which are of much value in salary discussions. Readers will receive valuable guidance on how to prepare for and conduct negotiations before accepting a new position.

Ding, Mae Lon. *Sources of Salary and Benefits for Job Seekers and Guidance Counselors.* Personnel Systems Associates, Tustin, CA, 1993.

A listing of sources of salary survey information. Strictly bibliographical in nature, meant to help the reader find sources of survey data. Surveys listed report average pay rates for different types of work.

Dukhut, Harold. *The Professional Resume & Job Search Guide.* Prentice Hall Press, New York, NY, 1981.

Strong focus on resume development for professionals, managers, and executives. Also provides valuable information on basic job search skills.

Fisher, Roger and William Ury. *Getting to Yes.* Penguin Books, New York, NY, 1985.

Simple, common sense advice which will strengthen the readers' negotiation skills. The ideas included in this book relate to position and salary negotiations.

Gerber, Michael E. *The E Myth.* Ballinger Publishing Co./Harper and Row Publishers, New York, NY, 1986.

Offers information on why most businesses don't work and what to do about it.

Germann, Richard and Peter Arnold. *Bernard Haldane Associates' Job and Career Building.* Harper and Row Publishers, New York, NY, 1980.

Sound information for getting started on a career search. Very easy to scan for information. Advice on resumes and interviewing is somewhat unconventional.

Hunt, Christopher W. and Scott A. Scanlon. *Directory of Human Resource Executives*. Hunt-Scanlon Publishing Co., Inc. Greenwich, CT, 1993

Includes 15,000 human resource professionals at 5,000+ leading public and private companies. Cross-indexed alphabetically, geographically, and by industry specialization. Includes in-depth career success articles by leaders in the field of human resources.

Lathrop, Richard. *Who's Hiring Who*. Ten Speed Press, Berkeley, CA, 1980.

Lathrop is noted for his unique approach to resumes (he calls them qualifications briefs), letters of application, and interviewing. (his approach is less than conventional.)

Lewis, Adele. *How to Write Resumes*. (2nd Ed.) Educational Series, Inc., Woodbury, New York, 1983.

A step-by-step approach to resume writing. Over 100 model resumes included. Tips on strategies for getting the job you want.

Miller, Arthur F. and Ralph T. Mattson. *The Truth About You*. Fleming H. Revell, Old Tappan, New Jersey, 1977.

A self-administered system for assessing knowledge, strengths, abilities, skills, and interests. (SIMA) System for Identifying Motivated Abilities. Good for career entry or change.

Molloy, John T. *Dress for Success*. Warner Books, New York, NY, 1975.

Molloy, John T. *The Women's Dress for Success Book*. Warner Books, New York, 1977.

Both have become classics on the "right" way to dress for creating the appropriate image both on the job and in the job search.

Petras, Ross and Kathryn. *The Only Job Hunting Guide You'll Ever Need*. Poseidon Press (Simon & Schuster), New York, NY, 1989.

One of the most complete and well-written sources of job hunting information assembled. Excellent how to guide for all levels and types of positions. Includes finding positions, writing resumes, interviewing, negotiations, references, and much more.

Shingleton, John D. and Robert Bao. *College to Career.* McGraw-Hill, New York, NY, 1977.

Provides a thorough and detailed source of career and job search information. Highly informative and readable. Good for college students and recent graduates.

Shingleton, John D. *Career Planning for the 1990's.* Garrett Park Press, Garret Park, MD., 1992.

Provides hard-hitting advice for developing career plans and carrying them out. Excellent guide for transition from college to career.

Snelling, Robert O. and Anne M. Snelling. *Jobs: What They Are... Where They Are... What They Pay.* Simon & Schuster, New York, NY, 1985.

A very complete guide that provides practical information on the total job search process.

Thompson, Melvin R. *Why Should I Hire You: How to Get the Job You Really Want.* Jove Publications, Inc., New York, NY, 1977.

Generally a useful book. Covers the job search from planning through follow-up. Areas especially useful are: resume preparation, interviewing via a referral system and negotiating offers.

APPENDIX F
NATIONAL ASSOCIATION OF
CAREER DEVELOPMENT CONSULTANTS

Robert C. Davenport
R. Davenport Associates
1901 Cochran Road
Suite 844, Manor Oak Two
Pittsburgh, PA 15220
(412) 561-4003

Joseph A. DiGiorgio
Human Resource Services
42202 Peach St., Suite 1,
Northwing
Erie, PA 16509-1358
(814) 868-4620

Rich Hollis
Resource Group Associates
1601 Northwest Expressway
Oklahoma City, OK 73119
(405) 848-8898

James Johnson
Executive Marketing Service
200 N. Warner Rd., Ste. 139
King of Prussia, PA 19406
(215) 992-0305

Gregory J. McCarthy
The Berkeley Corporation
2 Bala Plaza, Suite 714
Bala Cynwyd, PA 19004
(215) 644-3880

Richard T. Meyer, Chairman
Executive Transitions, Inc.
1655 North Fort Myer Dr.,
Suite 1150
Arlington, VA 22209
(703) 243-3838

John B. Millard
Millard Consulting Services
455 Pennsylvania Avenue
Fort Washington, PA 19034
(215) 646-0400

Louis Persico
Career Mgt Consultants, Inc.
3207 North Front Street
Harrisburg, PA 17110
(717) 233-2272

Clayton Rose
Clayton Rose Associates
27 Auburn Ct.
Red Bank, NJ 07701
(908) 758-1874

Grant Shannon
Merrill-Adams Associates
400 Lanidex Center
Parsippany, NJ 07054
(201) 884-2833

Euegene B. Shea
Eugene B. Associates, Inc.
800 Enterprise Drive, Suite 209
Oak Brook, IL 60521
(708) 573-4266

Robert C. Slayton
Slayton & Associates
1875 Lake Lila Lane,
Suite 13-B6
Ann Arbor, MI 48105
(313) 704-4357

Clare Stimson
Powersearch, Inc.
8888 Keystone Crossing Plaza,
Suite 700
Indianapolis, IN 46240
(317) 580-7000

Charles Timmins
Haven Scott Associates
145 Oak Hill Plaza
200 North Warner Road
King of Prussia, PA 19406
(215) 265-1714

David Werner
David Werner International, Inc.
420 Lexington Ave.
New York, NY 10170
(212) 682-8888

APPENDIX G
THIRD PARTY EMPLOYMENT SERVICES
(AGENCIES)

The Association for School, College and University Staffing (ASCUS) did a survey of Third Party Employment Services. The conclusions of the ASCUS membership were as follows:

1. Avoid an agency which is not affiliated with a professional association that possesses an established code of ethics and grievance procedures.

2. Work with those organizations who have at least two years of solid experience.

3. Avoid any organization which requests a payment of any kind before services are delivered.

4. Do not do business with a third party recruiter unless the recruiting agency has a written contract authorizing them to conduct a search on the client's behalf. In short, no contract, no business.

5. Inquire if the position is being filled in accordance with Equal Opportunity/Affirmative Action (Title VI, IX) guidelines. Rule of thumb: No EEO, no business.

Alumni placement offices that use the services of Third Party Employment Services (and many do not) will approximate these guidelines, although most university placement offices do not have written policies.

In the Midwest College Placement Association, a survey examining the nature of the interactions between Third Party Recruiters and placement offices, of 203 respondents, 176 reported having no printed policy.

Direction of communication between MCPA college members and TPES is unequal, one-sided, and incomplete. TPES adopt initiating stances while MCPA members adopt reactive positions. TPES wants cooperation from placement services but give little in return. Placement offices want ethical behavior and complete information regarding employment opportunities. At this time, no forum seems to exist to address these issues in an open, negotiatory manner.

Some TPES National Associations which possess a Code of Ethics and Grievance Procedures are:

Association of Executive Search Consultants
230 Park Avenue, Suite 1549
New York City, NY 10169
(212) 949-9556

National Association of Personnel Consultants*
3133 Mount Vernon Avenue
Alexandria, VA 22305

National Association of Teacher's Agencies
119 S. St. Asaph Street
Alexandria, VA 22314

National Association of Temporary Services*
119 S. Saint Asaph St.
Alexandria, VA 22314
(703) 549-6287

*Membership lists are available for purchase.

APPENDIX H
FORTY PLUS ORGANIZATIONS

Forty Plus is a group of non-profit, equal opportunity organizations consisting of men and women over the age of forty who are seeking career change. These autonomous organizations provide members with opportunities for networking, job search training, and support.

California

Forty Plus of No. California
7440 Lockheed Street
Oakland, CA 94614
(415) 430-2400

Forty Plus of So. California
Los Angeles Chapter
3450 Wilshire Blvd., Suite 510
Los Angeles, CA 90010
(213) 388-2301

Orange County Chapter
23172 Plaza Pointe Drive,
Suite 285
Laguna Hills, CA 92653
(714) 581-7990

Forty Plus of San Diego
4715 Viewridge Avenue
San Diego, CA 92123

Colorado

Forty Plus of Colorado
5800 West Alameda
Denver, CO 80226
(303) 937-4956

Northern Division
3840 S. Mason Street
Fort Collins, CO 80525
(303) 223-2470 Ext. 261

Southern Division
2555 Airport Road
Colorado Springs, CO 80910
(719) 473-6220 Ext. 271

Hawaii

Forty Plus of Hawaii
126 Queen Street, #227
Honolulu, HI 96813
(808) 531-0896

Illinois

Forty Plus of Chicago
28 East Jackson Boulevard
Chicago, IL 60604
(312) 922-0285

Minnesota

Forty Plus of Minnesota
14870 Granada Ave., Suite 315
St. Paul, MN 55124
(612) 683-9898

New York

Forty Plus of Buffalo
701 Seneca Street
Buffalo, NY 14210
(716) 856-0491

Forty Plus of New York
15 Park Row
New York, NY 10038
(212) 233-6086

Ohio

Forty Plus of Central Ohio
1100 King Avenue
Columbus, OH 43212-2203
(614) 275-0040

Pennsylvania

Forty Plus of Philadelphia
1218 Chestnut Street
Philadelphia, PA 19107
(215) 923-2074

Texas

Forty Plus of Dallas
13601 Preston Road, Suite 301
East Carillon Tower
Dallas, TX 75240
(214) 991-9917

Forty Plus of Houston
3935 Westheimer, #205
Houston, TX 77027
(713) 850-7830

Utah

Forty Plus of Utah
P.O. Box 11750
Salt Lake City, UT 84147-0750
(801) 533-2191

Washington

Forty Plus of Puget Sound
300 120th Avenue N.E.
Bldg. 7, Suite 200
Bellevue, WA 98005
(206) 450-0040

District of Columbia

Forty Plus of Greater Washington
1718 P Street, NW
Washington, DC 20036
(202) 387-1582

Index